WATERCRAFT PATROL
AND
SURVIVAL TACTICS

ABOUT THE AUTHORS

Don Turner graduated from the University of Arizona, and has worked for the Arizona Game and Fish Department for 16 years. His assignments have included Department Planner, Wildlife Manager, Law Enforcement Specialist, and Regional Supervisor. As a certified Arizona Peace Officer, he has performed watercraft patrol duties including patrols on the Salt and Colorado Rivers and their reservoirs. Turner is a Certified Public Manager, and has certifications in several fields, including firearms and watercraft. He has taught at the State Police Academy and helped prepare the State's watercraft officer training program. Current duties as a Regional Supervisor includes ten patrol watercraft and 26 peace officers. Don is a life member of the National Rifle Association, a member of the International Association of Law Enforcement Firearms Instructors, and the American Society of Law Enforcement Trainers.

Tony Lesce is a law enforcement journalist, and Associate Technical Editor of *Police Marksman* magazine. He has written for many of the principal law enforcement publications, including *Law and Order, Police, Police Marksman, Law Enforcement News, Police and Security News,* and others. He is the author of *"Police Product Handbook,"* and co-author with John Cheek of *"Plainclothes and Off-duty Officer Survival."*

WATERCRAFT PATROL
AND
SURVIVAL TACTICS

By

DONALD M. TURNER

Region VI Supervisor
Arizona Game and Fish Department

and

TONY LESCE

Associate Technical Editor
Police Marksman

CHARLES C THOMAS • PUBLISHER
Springfield • Illinois • U.S.A.

Published and Distributed Throughout the World by

CHARLES C THOMAS • PUBLISHER
2600 South First Street
Springfield, Illinois 62794-9265

© *1990 by* CHARLES C THOMAS • PUBLISHER

ISBN 0-398-05712-5

Library of Congress Catalog Card Number: 90-45356

With THOMAS BOOKS *careful attention is given to all details of manufacturing
and design. It is the Publisher's desire to present books that are satisfactory as to their
physical qualities and artistic possibilities and appropriate for their particular use.*
THOMAS BOOKS *will be true to those laws of quality that assure a good name
and good will.*

Printed in the United States of America
SC-R-3

Library of Congress Cataloging-in-Publication Data

Turner, Donald M.
    Watercraft patrol and survival tactics / by Donald M. Turner and
Tony Lesce.
        p.   cm.
    Includes bibliographical references and index.
    ISBN 0-398-05712-5 (cloth)
    1. Police patrol—Handbooks, manuals, etc. 2. Motorboats—
Handbooks, manuals, etc. I. Lesce, Tony. II. Title.
HV8080.P2T87   1990
363.2'32—dc20

                                                                            90-45356
                                                                            CIP

PREFACE

Policing afloat is very different from policing ashore and requires different tactics for officer survival. This book bridges the gap between watercraft patrol operations and watercraft patrol training with its focus on watercraft officer survival and tactics.

Although many agencies perform watercraft patrol and enforcement, there are few courses dealing with the specific training of watercraft patrol officers. Small boat operation and watercraft officer survival are not part of basic police academy training. Yet, it's not uncommon for a commander to give a new graduate the keys to a patrol boat, wishing him "good luck" as he leaves on his first patrol. For the most part, inexperienced officers are teamed with experienced watercraft patrol officers to "learn the ropes" without consideration of whether the experienced officer knows the right techniques to impart.

Police procedures and protection of constitutional liberties are the same for both land and water officers, but techniques of application vary greatly. One only has to remember his basic academy instruction on the proper way to control a suspect during a felony stop to realize that cars do not bob up and down, nor drift apart. On the water, the officer cannot order the felony suspect to exit his vehicle. These are examples of why watercraft enforcement requires a change in techniques and attitudes.

Nothing is as secure on the water as it is on land. Both equipment and tactics are different. Watercraft equipment is also much more expensive and the risks for damage greater.

As a new commander assigned to a unit with 10 patrol watercraft and up to 30 officers, the senior author (Turner) became very aware of his liabilities under the categories of "failure to train" and "failure to assign." It was necessary to develop lesson plans, using the experiences of older and wiser officers, and to provide a subordinate training program. Using this initial training and building on other sources, the Arizona Game and Fish Department decided to produce an agency-wide school for trainees who had completed the basic police academy, through the Arizona Boating Safety Program. This developed into a basic watercraft patrol officer school for training in-house cadets. With the approval of the Arizona Law Enforcement Officer Advisory Council, this school is now open to all enforcement agencies within the state of Arizona. Searching the literature showed that there's very little written on this topic, and that there is a need for a watercraft officer survival textbook.

This book deals with the threats faced by the watercraft patrol officer and how to cope with them so that the officer may finish his shift safely. We'll briefly describe various types of police agencies using water patrols, look at the different environments, and discuss both tactics and equipment appropriate to various situations.

Threats can be both personal and impersonal, intentional or inadvertent. Often, the officer encounters a wildlife law violator who is armed but not a hardened felon. His handling of the situation will determine whether or not it escalates into a violent encounter. Only rarely will a watercraft officer face an armed and dangerous felon, determined to resist arrest at all costs. This type of encounter is serious from the start, and the officer must know how to manage the incident to ensure his own safety.

Very commonly, the officer will find disorderly persons on the water. Some are simply recreational boaters violating speed or safety regulations. Others are public hazards, such as boaters creating large wakes in a no-wake zone. Many are under the influence of some sort of intoxicant, and the officer must recognize this and take special measures to ensure his safety and that of the public.

Although the authors wish to provide as detailed and comprehensive text as possible, we can't claim that this book covers everything there is to know about watercraft patrol and enforcement. Materials contained herein have come from an extensive pool of officer experiences beyond that of the Arizona Game and Fish Department. Due to the variety of laws, agency policies, water conditions, and watercraft configurations, we have limited our discussions to inland fresh water patrols utilizing 16 to 22 foot patrol boats.

Our terminology will be simple. When we use the word "suspect," we mean anyone who has committed or may have committed a felony or who may be armed and dangerous. It will also apply to anyone we have to arrest. We'll use the term "subject" for anyone not a suspect, including a person receiving a citation, and any other member of the public.

To avoid awkward phrasing, we'll use the pronoun "he" most often to describe an officer, subject, or suspect. We'll also use the terms "one-man" and "two-man" more often than "single-officer" and "double-officer," for brevity. We want the reader to understand that we recognize that females are playing increasingly important roles in watercraft law enforcement, both as officers and as suspects.

We hope that this book will assist the watercraft officer in the performance of his duties and alert him to the early warning signs of dangerous situations. We also hope that this book will stimulate instructors to develop increasingly safe and effective watercraft patrol tactics.

D.M.T.
T.L.

INTRODUCTION

There are many watercraft patrol officers stationed throughout the United States today. Some are assigned to inland freshwater enforcement, while others patrol coastal and ocean waterways. These officers work for city, county, state and federal agencies and have varying enforcement duties. Many are responsible for some type of environmental law enforcement, such as fishing, hunting, trapping, dumping, and pollution, while others are more oriented towards search and rescue operations.

Some are park police with limited enforcement authority. Yet others are sworn police officers with full enforcement powers, such as city police, sheriffs, and game wardens. All have similar responsibilities: the protection of the public and the public's property. Most are associated with some aspect of recreational boating safety enforcement. In some instances, other enforcement officers utilize the waterways as transportation during special operations. As their missions overlap, so do the techniques necessary to patrol water areas.

Watercraft patrol operations take place during daylight and nighttime hours, in good and bad weather and with one-man patrols or many-officer crews. Vessels range from canoes to hydroplanes and some have air support. Patrols may be routine, saturation, selective or special.

Not all patrol public contacts are with recreational boaters. Hostile watercraft operators, people under the influence of drugs or alcohol, anti-authority sociopaths, poachers, illegal dumpers, and smugglers are all potential threats. These types of encounters, as well as the risks created by environmental conditions, are part of the watercraft patrol task.

Individual officers have developed personal techniques to handle various problems. Likewise, agencies have produced training programs, procedures and policies to regulate and assist their officers in meeting and overcoming various situations they meet during watercraft patrol.

The authors have compiled ideas and tactics from many people and agencies in the preparation of this book. The techniques and procedures laid out in these pages do not, however, necessarily reflect those of any individual law enforcement agency, particularly those of the Arizona Game and Fish Department or the state of Arizona.

ACKNOWLEDGMENTS

The authors wish to thank all the watercraft patrol officers and support personnel who have contributed to watercraft survival skills.

Arizona Game and Fish Department:

John Adler, Tom Alexander, Henry Apfel, Richard Beaudry, Collins Cochran, Leonard Cooper, Dan Dymond, Barrett Edgar, Donna Erickson, Estevan Escobedo, Rick Gerhart, Bill Hansen, Mike Holloran, Ron Horejsi, Jack King, Ray Kohls, Tom Lister, Wes Martin, Dana McGehee, Leonard Ordway, Bill Ough, Mark Quigley, Richard Remington, Art Reynolds, Richard Rico, Eric Swanson, Larry Voyles, Tim Wade, Jim Warnecke, Larry Watt, John Werner and Rob Young.

Wildlife Manager Jim Fiedler who reviewed this manuscript and provided welcome input.

Frank Shoemaker, Senior Resident Agent, U.S. Fish & Wildlife Service, Mesa, Arizona.

Captain Dave Jordan and deputies, Gila County Sheriff's Lake Patrol, Arizona.

Doug Collup Park Manager and park rangers, Lake Pleasant, Maricopa County Parks and Recreation Department, Arizona.

Captain Jim Porter and deputies, Maricopa County Sheriff's Lake Patrol, Arizona.

Captains Mike Tucker and Ken Willoughby, Florida Marine Patrol, who developed the Marine Law Enforcement Skills, Tactics and Investigations Course for their agency. They also came and taught part of their course to watercraft officers of the Arizona Game and Fish Department in Phoenix, and they were good hosts to me while I was attending their training course in Tallahassee.

Jerry Scott, Ohio Department of Natural Resources.

Dan Maley, Loyd's Marine, Mesa, Arizona.

Jim Wilson, Sunset Boats, Phoenix, Arizona.

Finally, I would like to thank Duane Shroufe, Director of the Arizona Game and Fish Department, Tom Spalding, Deputy Director, and Lee Perry, Associate Director, for their support and encouragement of the Department's watercraft training and enforcement program.

CONTENTS

Page

Preface v

Introduction ix

PART I. WATERCRAFT ENFORCEMENT

Chapter

  1. Enforcement Authorities 5

  2. Water Safety Enforcement 11

  3. Water-Based Enforcement 21

  4. Patrol Efforts 27

  5. Search and Rescue 31

PART II. WATERCRAFT OFFICER SURVIVAL

  6. Survival Primer 35

  7. One- and Two-Officer Patrols 39

  8. Shoreline Contacts 45

  9. Campgrounds and Large Groups 51

10. Water Stops 55

11. Inspections 65

12. Stolen Boats 69

13. Arrests 73

14. Accident Responses 87

15. Night Operations 95

16. Booby Traps 105

17. Environmental Survival 107

18. Towing Watercraft 115

19. Assaults on the Water 119

PART III. WATERCRAFT PATROL EQUIPMENT

20. Officer Items 137

21. Watercraft Rigging 155
22. The Ideal Patrol Watercraft 191

PART IV. WATERCRAFT PATROL OFFICER TRAINING

23. Developing a Training Program 195
24. A Recommended Watercraft Patrol Officer Training Program . . . 205
25. Advanced Officer Training 265
Index 267

WATERCRAFT PATROL
AND
SURVIVAL TACTICS

PART I. WATERCRAFT ENFORCEMENT

Chapter 1

ENFORCEMENT AUTHORITIES

Americans love the water. From coast to coast, recreational boating and fishing are popular pastimes. Coupled with commercial waterway uses, we devote millions of hours a year to "on-water" activities.

Figure 1. Boating and fishing are two important recreational pursuits for Americans.

As a result of this popular form of recreation and livelihood, local, county, state, and federal lawmakers have authorized many public safety agencies to cope with the problems created by these activities.

Several levels of government employ thousands of people to monitor the use of our waterways. All 50 states, for example, have watercraft patrol and safety units. So do hundreds of cities and counties. Our federal government has several agencies dealing with water-related enforcement.

Figure 2. Many different types of government agencies are empowered to enforce watercraft regulations.

Patrols take place on streams, rivers, lakes, bays, sounds, canals, reservoirs, marshes, back waters, harbors, estuaries, intercoastal waters, coastal areas and marine environments.

Administered by the U.S. Coast Guard, millions of dollars have been allocated to the states for boating safety and enforcement programs. The budget for the Boating Safety Account for federal fiscal year 1989–1990 was $30 million. This money, coupled with state fees from boat registration, marine fuel taxes and other miscellaneous programs, provides the majority of funds for the nation's watercraft enforcement, education and safety effort.

As one can imagine, this has produced a variety of agencies, missions, policies and procedures for watercraft enforcement. Some water patrols concentrate on and are responsible for recreational boating. Some enforce

Figure 3. Various types of state agencies are responsible for boating safety and education.

Figure 4. County sheriff's offices also provide watercraft patrols.

just municipal ordinances. Some officers have limited enforcement authority while others have full police powers.

Enforcement patrols use vessels suited to their tasks, and these vessels range in size, expense and complexity from a single-officer kayak to large

Figure 5. Watercraft patrols take place on many types of waterways, from swamps to inland reservoirs.

crew serviced patrol craft. Tasks range from municipal enforcement, such as the protection of manatee breeding areas or "no docking" areas, all the way to interdiction of drug-smuggling operations. Between these extremes we find boating safety, operation, and registration, fishing, hunting, pollution, dumping and other recreational and criminal water-based enforcement duties. Officers also conduct search and rescue operations.

   In summary, watercraft patrol officers have been given the authority to protect the public safety and property, just as their fellow officers have on shore. The missions are basically the same, but, as we will discuss in this book, tactics, equipment and training are quite different.

Figure 6. Many agencies with watercraft patrol responsibilities are local as shown by this city patrol boat. They mainly enforce local ordinances.

Figure 7. Patrol boats must be suited for the water on which they patrol. Open boats are good for fair weather conditions but are inappropriate for cold and rough waters.

Figure 8. Watercraft patrol officers have the responsibility to protect the public on the water. Some recreational waterway users, such as these jet-skiers, at times appear to be their own worst enemies.

Figure 9. While on patrol, the watercraft officer may expect to see many different users of the waterway. These people flew in for an afternoon picnic.

Chapter 2

WATER SAFETY ENFORCEMENT

Laws and Regulations for Watercraft Safety

According to the National Association of State Boating Law Administrators' publication, *Small Craft Advisory* (August–September, 1989), during 1988, 5,836 boating collisions resulted in 167 fatalities. There were also 608 capsizings with 305 fatalities, and 450 falls overboard with 260 fatalities. All occurred on this country's waterways. In other words, the most common type of accident is a collision with another boat and the most common fatal accident is a capsizing or fall overboard.

In order to prevent these casualties to life and property, there have been many laws and regulations passed by legislative bodies. Watercraft patrol officers are responsible for enforcing these laws and educating the public. Their job is to reduce the potential damages by their presence and by skillful detection and apprehension of violators.

Most of the boating laws revolve around three basic areas:

1. Watercraft registrations, numbering systems and taxes
2. Watercraft safety equipment
3. Watercraft operation

As with motor vehicle registrations, there are two reasons for registering watercraft. One is boat and owner identification, and the other is revenue generation. A watercraft officer inspecting registrations benefits the public in several ways. In making public contacts, he checks records and watercraft hull identification numbers (HIN), conducts safety equipment inspections, and oversees safe boating. Such routine enforcement produces a ripple effect.

Boaters tell their friends that they were stopped, officers order unsafe boats off the water, and other boaters have a good excuse to bring their registrations up to date and ensure that their equipment is serviceable. The worst that can happen is for the public to believe their favorite area is unpatrolled. No matter how upright people are, the active watercraft patrol provides the motivation for public compliance.

One successful technique used by the Arizona Game and Fish Depart-

Figure 1. Regular stops and inspections, such as this boating safety check, lets the public know that officers enforce laws on the water. The high profile reduces safety violations and provides motivation for compliance with regulations.

ment is to set up a check station at the public entrance of a large popular reservoir. Several officers interview the drivers of vehicles towing boats through the station. Officers check boats on trailers for registration, safety equipment and HINs. Operators whose boats fail safety equipment or registration checks are advised of their violation and given advice on how to comply with the legal requirements. Officers advise them emphatically that they may not operate their boats without compliance.

As a routine precaution against violators' ignoring the advice, officers radio their registration numbers to a watercraft patrol boat on the reservoir. Suspicious registration paperwork or HIN numbers results in the immediate seizure of the boat, or a written referral for a follow-up investigation.

Approximately 10 percent of the boats checked resulted in a follow-up investigation, while 30 percent failed the registration or safety equipment checks. During the 1989 watercraft season, officers used this technique on three major reservoirs in the central part of the state with approximately the same results at each station. As officers had expected, a couple of boaters at each station did not believe the friendly advice they were given. Instead, they launched their boats and received personal invitations to explain their derelictions to the local justice of the peace.

Water Safety Equipment

All states and the federal government, through the U.S. Coast Guard, have enacted laws requiring minimal safety equipment for watercraft. These vary from state to state, and equipment required varies with the type of boat.

Figure 2. Regardless of the type of boat, most states have regulations governing their use and safety equipment.

Most specify that required safety equipment be readily available. Reports of boating fatalities show that most fatal accidents could have been prevented if the boat users had been wearing personal flotation devices (life jackets—PFDs).[1] A watercraft patrol officer should be well-versed in safety equipment inspection. Subjects violating safety regulations must be brought into compliance immediately for their own protection. An officer will make a serious mistake if he feels that overlooking an equipment problem or giving a warning without further action is adequate enforcement. An officer who ignores violations, such as relating to PFDs or fire extinguishers, may be judged liable for any accidents that may occur immediately after his inspection. Probably the best response is to issue the responsible party a citation and remove the unsafe boat from the water until the owner corrects the safety problem. Without a supporting citation, some subjects have complained that the officer's ordering them off the water to correct a safety problem was "harassment." The citation itself is the best defense for such a complaint.

There are many books regarding safety equipment for boats. It's enough to say here that each watercraft patrol officer must know both his local laws and his agency's procedures for detecting and correcting unsafe equipment problems. Equipment checks should be a routine part of any stop. An officer who always checks for registration and safety equipment with every stop has built a solid base for any challenges in court for his actions which have resulted in a citation or arrest.

Watercraft Operation

Besides enforcing laws regarding registration and equipment, the watercraft patrol officer must be constantly alert for violations of the "operation laws." Whether a boat operator is a seasoned "salt" or a novice, there are very specific laws regulating his actions on the water. These laws range from "operation under the influence" (O.U.I.), reckless operation, and noise regulations, to navigation rules. These laws, like the motor vehicle traffic code, are to reduce boating accidents by providing a safe boating environment.

In some jurisdictions, enforcement procedures place a higher priority on the enforcement of "operation" laws than registration and equipment. This is because violation of operation rules creates a very dangerous situation for the public and results in some spectacular and deadly accidents. There are many facets of the operation regulations, and watercraft patrol officers have devised various techniques to deal with them.

"Let's go fishin', I'll buy the bait and get the boat ready, why don't you bring a case of beer?" is one way the day begins for some fishermen. Daily, boaters consume tremendous volumes of alcohol while enjoying their favorite outdoor sport. Because many accept alcohol as part of the boating recreation experience, even some legislators don't take seriously the negative effects of alcohol consumption while boating. Adding drugs to the alcohol problem creates a deadly combination that impairs judgment and coordination.

Under the law, "Operating Under the Influence" (O.U.I.) means that a boat operator's ability to operate his vessel is impaired. For example, some state laws define "impairment to the slightest degree" as unacceptable. Various legal bodies have defined impairment by linking blood chemistry or coordination tests to operator performance. The study, apprehension and testing for O.U.I. of motor vehicle operators has become a detailed science. However, for the watercraft patrol officer, many of the "probable-cause" reasons for detection of O.U.I. motor vehicles do not pertain to watercraft operation. For instance, a motor vehicle operator who drives on or over the centerline presents the motor officer with a high degree of probability that the operator is O.U.I. Lakes and rivers do not have painted lines, and water enforcement officers must find other means of detecting drunks or impaired operators.

Alcohol is a central nervous system depressant. With the consumption of alcohol a boat operator's judgment becomes impaired. The boater loses his sense of caution, becomes a risk taker, is overconfident of his abilities, and is unaware of errors or omissions. Alcohol also degrades visual acuity, reaction time, speed, balance and coordination. Intoxication affects vision and reaction time first.

Aggravating the problem is the operator's increased exposure. The recreational watercraft operator is not as protected from the environment as he would be in a motor vehicle. Very few watercraft provide air conditioning, protection from the wind, or protection from the sun. Operating on the water exposes people directly to the effects of the environment. Although dehydration normally occurs while on the water, alcohol consumption aggravates it, and the water loss enhances the alcohol's effects. The sun's direct and reflected glare strain the eyes, and if they are already impaired from consumption, the effects are greater. Some studies have shown that four hours on a boat is equivalent to .10 blood alcohol level in effects on reaction time and judgment.[2]

The statistics for 1988 show that of the 5,836 boating collisions recorded, 70 percent were found to be the fault of the operator. Visibility was good to fair during 80 percent of the accidents.[3]

Usually, watercraft patrol officers detect O.U.I. while investigating an accident or while observing a blatant operation violation. Yet, we suspect that many, of boat users are impaired from consuming alcohol. As we've seen, O.U.I. is not as easy to detect on the water as it is on the street.

Traditional techniques of impairment analysis, such as coordination checks, are extremely difficult, if not impossible, to do in a bobbing boat.

Heel-to-toe, closed eyes nose touching, and similar coordination tests are sometimes inconclusive due to the motion of the boat. Many times a watercraft patrol officer must take the subject to shore to perform the coordination tests. Breath analyzers show breath alcohol levels, but in many jurisdictions watercraft laws do not require boaters to submit to breath analyzer testing.

There are three techniques which do help the watercraft patrol officer with impairment tests. First, even though it is difficult to perform motor coordination tests on the water, mental coordination tests may also serve as evidence. Tests such as finger counting, repeating sentences after the officer, alphabet recitation, and number counts, are good techniques to apply aboard boats. Second, portable intoximeters are available. When these become more reliable and less costly, their simplicity and portability will make them an excellent tool for the watercraft officer. Third, the Horizontal Gaze Nystagmus (HGN) technique is currently the best field impairment test offered. It takes three days of training to learn, and the officer must establish his expertise before his test is acceptable in court.

The main advantage of the HGN test is that it can be used anywhere. As alcohol consumption directly affects visual control, HGN tests the function of the eye muscles during a simple visual tracking exercise. Experienced officers apply this technique reliably and find it an important tool to remove impaired operators from streets and waterways. Currently, this is the most practical technique for watercraft officers.

One enforcement tactic is to set up several boater sobriety check points on major bodies of water during the watercraft season. Several watercraft enforcement officers, certified in HGN, man a pontoon boat. Other officers direct suspected boaters to the pontoon boat for testing.

Recently, Sgt. Gerald Kersey of the Georgia Department of Natural Resources completed a review of 173 boating-under-the-influence arrests made in that state. Over a 14-month period, Sgt. Kersey found that 97% of the suspects were white males, and 56% were 26 to 35 years old. Operationally, 58.4% were stopped between 6 P.M. and 10 P.M., and 14% of the arrests were made after an accident or during a safety inspection. Blood alcohol levels ran from .11% to .15% (although the sergeant reported that two were at .25% and .27%), and 2% were on drugs.[4]

Operating under the influence of illegal drugs is just as serious as alcohol. Tests for drug impairment are basically the same as for alcohol, but the blood alcohol or breath analyzer tests are negative because they don't detect these drugs. The HGN test is also useful for detection of

PCP use, because this drug is a central nervous system depressant. Even without a formal test, a watercraft officer might observe his subjects using illegal substances, subjecting the boat to seizure and potential confiscation.

Driving 60 miles per hour through a residential area with a motor vehicle is dangerous and reckless, and so are many ways to operate a boat. Even though many regulations specify the legal ways to operate boats, they don't prevent misuse of waterways. Actions such as bow riding, creating excessive wake, operating in a swimming area, overloading, running at night without lights, operating contrary to traffic patterns, reckless towing of skiers, etc., are examples of reckless operation. Depending on local conditions and circumstances, a watercraft patrol officer may determine such operation to be criminal endangerment. The operator is liable for his actions, especially if such operation leads to loss of life or property.

Figure 3. Creating an excessive wake in a prohibited area is an operation violation. Enforcing this regulation contributes to public safety on the water.

The watercraft patrol officer must always be watchful for this type of violation and must stop and correct the violator. Of all duties, this one receives the most public concern and scrutiny, because it is very high-profile enforcement. Not only must an officer be able to stop such violations, but his seamanship skills will be tested as he must overtake and apprehend these subjects without risking personal and public safety.

Boats operated without adequate muffling devices are public nuisances because they ruin almost everyone's peace and quiet. Many states, such as Arizona, have noise and muffling regulations. Ineffective and inoperable muffling devices are illegal. Mufflers must be in operation and must reduce the noise level to a specified limit. In Arizona, a watercraft must not emit noise louder than 86 decibels on the weighted "A" scale. The sound must be measured by a calibrated device placed at least 50 feet from the engine. This noise restriction only applies once a boat is on plane.

Of all the public complaints received by the department, noise is one of the most frequent. Because of the law's requirements, Arizona watercraft patrol officers must complete a training course on sound meter calibration and use. Most successful "noise" patrols employ an undercover watercraft to take readings and one or two marked chase patrol boats. "Hog boats" running dry stacks are stopped for violations, and boating inspections also include checks for flame arrestors, scoops and muffling devices.

Throughout the United States, there are various devices designed to aid boaters in navigating the waterways safely. These include buoys, steel or concrete structures, lighthouses, radio beacons, radar reflectors, range lights, etc. Most appear on waterway charts.

The watercraft patrol officer finds these devices helpful. One use is to avoid hazards and to determine his position. The watercraft patrol officer must also ensure that the boating public obeys these devices. In some areas, the patrol officer must maintain them. Regardless of responsibility, patrol officers should make sure that damaged, missing or non-functioning navigational aids are repaired. In some instances, the officer may have to make repairs himself.

Every watercraft patrol officer must be intimately familiar with all navigation aids on his patrol beat. He must know where each is located, its size, shape, and purpose. He must also know whether each is operating properly. The officer might even have to submit recommendations for their type and placement, or replacement.

Other regulations affecting watercraft operations are navigational rules, also known as "rules of the road." These specify rights of way, direction of travel and other "traffic" laws designed to promote safe and orderly boat operation.

Figure 4. Some jurisdictions have regulations regarding the maximum noise a boat engine can make. An officer uses a sound meter to measure the sound level of a suspected violation.

NOTES

1. 1988 Boating Accidents, *Small Craft Advisory,* August–September, 1989, pages 10–12, and videotape, "The Reasons People Drown," Dr. Frank Pia, LSA.
2. Class Notes, Florida Marine Patrol, *Marine Law Enforcement Skills, Tactics, and Investigations,* Tucker & Willoughby, 1988.
3. *Small Craft Advisory,* 1989.
4. Ibid., p. 13.

Chapter 3

WATER–BASED ENFORCEMENT

As well as promoting boating safety, a watercraft officer's responsibility covers other violations that occur on and near waterways, including felonies. Many of these violators assume the guise of recreational boaters to cover their operations.

1. Stolen Boats

Although stolen boats are a nationwide problem, they don't receive as much legislative concern as do stolen motor vehicles. Manufacturers cannot agree on the type and placement of identification markings on boats. There's also no consistent state-to-state requirement that boats must have titles for registration.

The problem's severity varies from one jurisdiction to another. Some states, such as Arizona, do not require a title to register a watercraft, although they do require titles for motor vehicles. This allows easy "laundering" of stolen boats through and from that state. Another convenience for the boat thief is that U.S. Coast Guard regulations require that the boat be registered in the state of "principal use," not the state of residence of the owner. Another inconsistency is that some states assess the boats as property, while others do not.

Tracking stolen boats is much more difficult than tracking stolen vehicles. Penalties for destruction of a hull identification number (HIN) vary from state to state and the ways of placing hidden HINs vary between manufacturers.

All boats manufactured in the United States have been required to have a HIN since 1972, a result of the Federal Boating Safety Act of 1971, which requires HINs on all non-commercial boats. Generally, this definition comprises recreational boats up to 65 feet long. However, the industry is not as well regulated as the one for motor vehicles.

An aggravating factor in boat thefts is that many states do not require inspection of a HIN before registration. Compounding the problem is that there are about 5,000 manufacturers, although 80 percent of small boats come from slightly over 100 companies. Additionally, some jurisdictions do not require owners to allow peace officers to inspect the HINs unless the boat is actually on the water.

In Arizona, the outcomes of several boat seizures show the difficulties of investigating and prosecuting boat thefts. Most had a paper trail so tangled (changes of ownership, lack of a victim, lack of a police report, and multiple state registrations) that a probable-cause complaint was impossible to obtain from the prosecuting attorney. This resulted in seized boats with altered or obliterated HINs being returned as "legal" boats. Often, the boat's current owner doesn't know that the boat he purchased was stolen, because the paperwork he sees is valid. Professional boat thieves are operating watercraft versions of "chop shops," and converting stolen boats to legitimate ones, to sell in Arizona and probably in other states, as well. Rarely do they operate stolen boats, with the slight risk of detection. However, it's likely that watercraft officers regularly board and inspect stolen boats without detecting the violation.

2. *Drugs, Contraband and Smuggling*

Our "war on drugs" takes place in the air, on the sea, on land, AND on our inland waterways. As Arizona's border with California and Nevada is the Colorado River, Arizona peace officers have received information that dope smugglers have shifted some of their transportation routes to the river to reduce the risk of being interdicted by city, county, and state narcotics officers.

At a large and crowded lake near metropolitan Phoenix, an informant told game and fish officers that, while night fishing, he had heard engine noises from the side of the lake that had no land access. Upon investigating, officers determined that the noise came from a generator providing power to a water pump being used to irrigate a camouflaged marijuana field near the lake. The grower evidently had set up and supplied that operation by boat.

There has long been use of narcotics and other contraband by recreational boaters. On the water, far from other people and free from observation, most dope users feel confident that their activities will go undetected. Occasionally, these people will attract others with similar recreational interests and form large "rafts" of boats. They bring drugs with them or arrange for their transport. From recreational users, to smugglers, to suppliers, drugs are often present on our patrolled waterways.

3. *Crimes Against Property*

As on land, crimes against property are common on our waterways. Watercraft officers regularly investigate complaints of vandalism of docks, marinas, boats and natural resources. Other property crimes entail theft of boating equipment and even theft of boat registration decals.

People steal in surprising circumstances. One watercraft officer returned to his patrol boat to discover that two of his PFDs were missing. Later on that day, during a boating inspection, he found his PFDs, much to his happiness and to the suspect's dismay. When questioned, the suspect said that he took them because he didn't want to operate his boat without the right number of PFDs! He had not realized that they were marked with the officer's badge and agency identification numbers. Every sort of material object is vulnerable to theft or other crimes against property.

4. *Crimes Against Persons*

These crimes are fairly common on and near our waterways. Shootings, stabbings, assaults, and rapes, in campgrounds next to swimming and launching areas, are frequent occurrences.

During one memorable incident, which occurred on an Easter weekend, an outlaw biker gang obtained a permit for campground use next to a lake near Phoenix. The affair was orderly until members of a rival outlaw biker gang infiltrated the party. After several fights and stabbings, someone notified the authorities. Among the four sheriff's deputies in the area, two were watercraft patrol officers. However, game and fish rangers were conducting a special patrol that weekend, and six watercraft patrol officers found themselves manning a roadblock with riot guns. Both agencies stood their ground, to keep the two rival gangs apart, until reinforcements arrived a couple of hours later.

Many watercraft officers know of similar incidents and probably have investigated these type of crimes. We don't have to stretch the imagination to know that felony enforcement is almost routine. The prospect of encountering a felon in the act or after the fact is a realistic probability for watercraft officers.

5. *Accident Investigations*

Boating accident investigations comprise a significant part of a watercraft patrol officer's duties. Several very good training programs provide techniques to help officers become proficient in accident investigation and accident reconstruction. As in a criminal investigation, the accident investigator must interview witnesses, collect and preserve evidence, and take good notes. Compounding the problem is that unlike motor vehicle accidents, boats are moved or sunk and conditions have changed when the investigator begins his work.

Figure 1. Not all accidents involving watercraft occur on the water. This early departure from the trailer falls under the "OOPS" category.

In an accident investigation, the watercraft officer is actually performing four tasks: receiving notification of the accident, planning the investigation, conducting the investigation, and analyzing the evidence he develops. He may issue complaints after completing the analysis.

The officer should be sure to contact other agencies with concurrent responsibilities. This is professional courtesy, which will help get reciprocal assistance when needed. Providing needed information to other agencies is made easier by standardized reporting forms. Most states have a standardized form and format to follow.

There is a standard array of investigative tools that officers should keep in their patrol boats. You'll find a list of these in Chapter 19.

6. Warrant Arrests

Suspects with outstanding warrants are often involved in recreational boating, and "warrant hits" are fairly frequent, which is why the watercraft officer must be mentally and physically prepared to make a full custody arrest. We'll discuss tactical and survival techniques for dealing with this on a patrol boat later in this book.

7. Hunting, Trapping, Fishing and Environmental Laws

Fishermen are very common in recreational boating, and almost all boaters fish at one time or another. A fishing license check is a good introduction to a boating inspection. Because fishing regulations may vary greatly, even between various bodies of water, a watercraft officer needs a solid grounding in conservation enforcement, whether he's a "game warden" or not.

Figure 2. Fishermen contacts while on watercraft patrol are frequent, and a watercraft officer should be well versed in the fishing and hunting regulations which cover his patrol area.

Another common user of the waterways is the hunter. Some animals lend themselves to being hunted with a boat. Waterfowl hunting is the most obvious, but many times a favorite quail area might be reachable only via boat. Trappers also utilize boats to set and check trap lines.

Again, a good watercraft officer must have a thorough knowledge of the fish and game regulations as they're relevant to activities in his patrol area.

You can expect all hunters and trappers to be armed. Although laws concerning prohibited weapons, prohibited possessors, or concealed weapons vary between states, it's not unusual to see pistols in tackle boxes or shotguns on the deck. People bring firearms into camps and unfortunately are not always wise or careful with them. There have been instances in which watercraft officers have had to respond to "man with a weapon" calls at public campgrounds.

There are other conservation and environmental laws that affect waterways, such as dumping, polluting, woodcutting (transport to and from by boat) and littering. In Arizona most of our central lakes are on U.S. Forest Service land and because the reservoirs are dammed streams, there are many American Indian historical sites in the area. It is a violation of state and federal law to excavate these sites, but "pot hunters" are plentiful. Access to many of these sites is by boat. As with other enforcement categories, the watercraft officer must be familiar with the laws governing archaeological site preservation. When theft of artifacts is a felony, watercraft officers represent authority, and violators see them as adversaries regardless of the type of crime.

Chapter 4

PATROL EFFORTS

Patrol is the watercraft officer's most common enforcement duty. There are several types of patrols, and their conduct and tactical techniques vary with the objectives.

1. Routine Patrols

One or more officers operate a patrol boat, frequently highly visible, in a fairly random pattern while contacting as many boaters as possible. This is the "fly the flag" type of patrol which demonstrates to the public that the agency is doing its job. It also places patrol watercraft to be in their natural role: on the water and available for response.

Basic reconnaissance may be part of the mission. Checking out water conditions, safety areas, problem areas and navigation devices are all routine patrol functions.

The worst error for a patrol officer to make is to leave the mooring without a good idea of what he'll be doing that day. All patrol efforts should have a pre-planned objective, despite the prospect of response to calls and other problems obstructing the original objectives. A trap to avoid is to fall into routine habits, the result of complacency arising from mental laziness. An officer must constantly ensure that he varies his patrol times, routes and areas. Getting into a rut is boring, non-productive and potentially dangerous. It also prevents the patrol officer from acquiring a complete perspective of his patrol area.

As with the military, an officer on patrol also gathers "intelligence," or information. He observes what is going on in his patrol area, as well as the people involved in various activities. He remains alert to any problems that may be occurring. He notes any shifts in recreational use and becomes aware of public concerns. He also inspects for potential or actual safety problems. "Routine patrol" is an effective way to cope with these and other problems.

When routine patrol uncovers problems that officers can't correct through routine patrol techniques, they coordinate with other patrol

Figure 1. The watercraft patrol officer should have his day well planned before leaving the harbor.

units or ask for help from supervisors. Getting help can often correct a problem officers cannot handle by themselves.

2. Saturation Patrols

These are intensifications of routine patrol, bringing together several patrol boats and officers at the same time and place to make as many public contacts as possible during a limited time. The intent is to increase the efforts of the regular patrol and to impress upon the public the agency's commitment to safe boating practices.

3. Selective Enforcement Patrols

Designed to solve a variety of special problems, these patrols usually target a specific violation. They may require the use of specialized personnel and resources, including some from other agencies. Such a patrol may be an effort against O.U.I. suspects on a waterway where routine patrol has revealed that these violations are common. A selective enforcement patrol for O.U.I. might require a centralized processing area, several marked patrol watercraft and officers, and several unmarked or undercover watercraft. Additionally, the effort may require officers who are certified in special O.U.I. testing techniques, such as HGN. There may also have to be a special communications net and a press officer to coordinate press releases. The agency may also seek help from the local enforcement agency for prisoner control and transport, thus allowing watercraft officers to continue their patrols.

Other selective patrols can be effective against nighttime violations, organized fishing operations, noise regulation, safety equipment requirements and even registration compliance. A patrol supervisor must strive to maintain the integrity of a selective enforcement operation, because it's easy for officers to revert to routine patrol techniques. General Bruce Clarke, U.S. Army, once said: "An organization does well only those things the boss checks." For those officers in command of a selective patrol, those words are certainly true, and the operation's success may directly depend on the ability to maintain an intensive effort.

Normally, selective enforcement patrols provide for no discretion. Routine warnings and "breaks" procedures should be suspended for the operation. With much equipment and many officers devoted to apprehending suspects, anything less than a citation for a direct violation of the law is wasted effort.

4. Special Patrols

Organized to fill a void in the routine patrol effort, special patrols concentrate on assisting regular watercraft officers with their patrol mission. For instance, on special holiday weekends, special patrols of officers may be assigned to a waterway to assist regularly assigned patrol officers. In Arizona, as well as in some other states, there aren't enough officers to provide adequate coverage on holidays.

One type of special patrol designed to cope with this problem is the transfer of resources from other waters unaffected by the holiday volume. Another expedient is for experienced watercraft patrol officers assigned to staff jobs to leave their desks for a couple of days on the water. Another tactic is to have three patrol watercraft work overlapping shifts on a waterway. This allows for patrol coverage of 20 hours with two-boat overlaps during the busiest periods.

5. Patrol Evaluations

Continuing evaluations of all patrols—routine, saturation, selective and special—allow the supervisor to apply his resources effectively. The patrol leader must note the problems encountered and evaluate the patrols' effectiveness. He must also appraise manpower and logistics and solicit feedback from patrol officers to include in his after-action report.

This is especially true for saturation and special patrols, to provide a record of accomplishment. More importantly, they can stimulate recommendations regarding what to do next time to make the operation more efficient and effective.

Chapter 5

SEARCH AND RESCUE

Watercraft officers, whatever their regular duties, sooner or later become involved in search and rescue operations. Many agencies have highly equipped and trained search and rescue units. However, search and rescue responsibilities vary from state to state depending on local laws and needs.

Statutes don't regulate everything, though. A watercraft officer in a state which delegates search and rescue to others will find that the public expects assistance from him regardless. Realistically, the watercraft patrol officer is going to be involved in search and rescue, sometimes simply because he's first on the scene.

As we all know, bodies of water can be quite hazardous. Clear and calm lakes can turn into whitecap nightmares in minutes. Good seamanship and a knowledge of first-aid techniques, coupled with a basic component of emergency equipment, are essential for all watercraft patrol officers.

Although we all wish that "searches" end with "rescues," many do not. Lost victims in boating accidents provide much prolonged grief for their loved ones, who remain uncertain about their fate. This is why body recovery is important.

There are many techniques for body searches, but a very innovative one involved bringing in dogs to seek out a drowning victim at Saguaro Lake in Arizona. In the Spring, 1989 issue of the *International Game Warden* magazine, the editor writes about a conversation he had with a Georgia deputy warden whose dog was trained to detect human bodies underwater. This technique originated in the United States and is relatively new. It's worth keeping in mind in case of a protracted search for a drowning victim.

PART II. WATERCRAFT OFFICER SURVIVAL

Chapter 6

SURVIVAL PRIMER

Tactics for officer survival on the water are radically different from survival tactics for the streets. The main purpose is, nevertheless, for the officer to control the situation from the start of the contact to the end and to emerge unharmed. Studies show that about 85 percent of the contacts with recreational boaters are not the result of violations. We stress this because you should always remember this, and base your actions on good tactics and sound public relations, to avoid escalating a non-confrontational contact.

A positive attitude is important. This means that you must be prepared to take whatever steps are necessary to ensure your safety. This includes developing good tactics and maintaining your equipment. You must also be prepared to consider new ideas. If you keep an open mind, you'll then be ready to adopt techniques to enhance your personal safety. This survival attitude applies to training as well as procurement, utilization, deployment, and maintenance of equipment. It even extends to physical and environmental factors of the patrol area. Every task can be accomplished better, easier and safer if you keep an innovative and questioning mind. If you develop a positive survival attitude, you'll also read, study, practice, train, innovate, and use common sense. Let's look at this a bit more:

The topic of officer survival is composed of three items, oftentimes called the "survival triangle." This involves the three elements of MENTAL/PHYSICAL CONDITIONING, TACTICS, and SHOOTING SKILL.[1] Perhaps a better way to picture it is as an attitude that we can diagram as a square of four sides which include the three skills plus another one representing KNOWLEDGE. In the middle of this square would be the words POSITIVE MENTAL ATTITUDE. Of all survival factors, a positive mental attitude is at the center and is the most important of all.

You must also understand clearly that if you are ignorant of the dangers posed by your working environment and how to overcome them, then this degrades your survival skills. Jerry Scott of the Ohio

Division of Wildlife calls the desire to survive as "PSI" for Personal Survival Instinct. Regardless of how you describe or discuss it, officer survival relates directly to you and your desire to live and return home. You must be willing to learn, practice and be aware of your work environment. Only your attitude will make the difference.

Another important aspect of a positive survival attitude is control of your emotions. You've surely noticed that some members of the public can be very irritating (especially if they are drunk and insulting), others are just naturally abrasive, and some are cop-haters. If you allow yourself to be provoked by someone with a chip on his shoulder, you can lose control of your emotions and of the situation. This can escalate a contact to a dangerous degree. It's important for you to understand that a public contact, or even a confrontation, is not a personal contest. You get no points for being "Supercop." On the other hand, there are smart ways and hard ways of handling such encounters. You also must learn to recognize a "no-win" situation and get out of it until you can summon enough resources to handle it.

Also important is the development of good survival skills. Much of this is good judgment and learning to recognize the cues that signal danger. Learning to identify hostile environments will go a long way towards keeping you out of trouble.

A positive attitude leads to good habits and a good habit is to avoid the "Five Deadly Sins," adapted from Pierce Brooks's book on officer survival, *Officer Down, Code Three.* The deadly survival sins are:

CARELESSNESS. This means neglecting to remain alert, observing the situation, and taking proper precautions. You can be careless by prejudging a suspect or situation. If you become sloppy, you may allow a suspect to control the events and take control from you.

FAILURE TO PLAN AHEAD. If you let events overtake and overwhelm you, you've failed to plan ahead. Going into a situation without appraising it is that sort of failure. Not using high ground or other features to tactical advantage is also failure to plan.

DISREGARD FOR PERSONAL SAFETY. Pierce Brooks calls this "Tombstone Courage." If you allow yourself to be carried away into a personal contest with subjects, not realizing that discretion is often the better part of valor, you're gambling. If you fail to utilize backup and feel that your skills and "guts" are enough to overcome the situation, you're risking everything on a very shaky assumption.

FAILURE TO COMMUNICATE. This impairs the superiority you usually have over subjects. Organization makes up for the elements of surprise and individual initiative, advantages some offenders often have over individual officers. Failure to communicate means not just the official radio net, but to communications with fellow officers and even partners. Often, partners will discuss social events, and make other small talk, but won't discuss what they will do in a serious situation. If you fail to communicate, you sabotage your organizational superiority and you endanger your partner and perhaps other officers.

FAILURE TO CONTROL THE SITUATION. This is the deadly end result of the other four failures and omissions. This is the bottom line, the one which gets officers injured and killed.

Finally, remember that officer survival goes beyond prevailing in a punch-out or a shoot-out. As a law officer, you bear a burden of responsibility that the suspect does not. You have to observe legal guidelines on use of force, and your responsibility continues through the suspect's trail. At times, it may appear that you have to balance too many conflicting requirements to do your job properly, but the reputation of your agency, your welfare, and that of your family all depend upon how you handle yourself when the crisis comes. Also remember that "survival" takes in your economic, physical, and emotional well-being.

NOTES

1. *Street Survival,* Calibre Press, 1980.

Chapter 7

ONE- AND TWO-OFFICER PATROLS

Deployment

In many jurisdictions, there's not enough manpower to deploy water-craft patrol officers in two-man patrols for every waterway. This is why, for the most part, these patrol officers work alone. Officers may occasionally be paired up during high-risk activities, such as selective or special patrols. One effect of this is that, unless the patrol officer has the same partner each time, it is difficult to develop a "team" approach.

Other jurisdictions provide for two-man watercraft patrol operations. In this case, officers have the opportunity to know each other and develop team techniques.

Additionally, commanders may decide to use one-man patrols in some situations and two-man patrols in others. An example is when an officer calls in sick and the commander has to split a team to cover the sector.

Differences in Risks and Assaults

Two-man teams appear to face greater risks. There are several reasons for this. Commanders tend to use one-officer watercraft patrol units in low-risk situations, or on low-risk missions to obtain maximum coverage. They tend to assign two-man teams to high-risk situations and locales, because they know the extra help is necessary. Officers working in pairs may become overconfident and take unnecessary risks; they get a false sense of security. Also, one may neglect an essential task because he assumes that his partner is taking care of it; this is one of the "Five Deadly Sins"—failure to communicate.

Working Alone

If you're on solitary patrol, you must learn to be self-sufficient and use personal initiative in both vital issues and minor details. There is no one around to lend you a set of batteries if your flashlight goes dead. If you don't perform necessary maintenance, nobody else will. When on patrol, you're on your own and cannot depend on anyone for help. You'll have to learn to analyze all contacts before the approach. You'll also need to develop an acute internal warning system to highlight unsafe situations.

Figure 1. Working alone can make simple jobs difficult. The individual officer must learn to be self-reliant and develop a routine for each task.

You'll have to modify your techniques for your safety. You'll need to be very careful to scan hull numbers before getting in close, and you'll probably want to conduct all inspections from your boat, instead of boarding the other one, especially if there are several people on board the other boat. You may ask the operator to pass his fire extinguisher and PFDs over to you for inspection, instead of boarding his boat for a close look.

You'll also have to develop techniques of seamanship, using only your two hands, for which you'd normally use four. You'll find it harder to perform some tasks, such as boarding inspections. You'll have to control your boat, inspect the other boat, answer questions, look out for weapons and watch your back simultaneously. On the other hand, you have much personal freedom. You set your daily schedule and route. You maintain your own equipment and you don't have to worry about a partner's dependability, or lack thereof. You're also personally responsible for your actions.

Always, always, always maintain good communications with your radio dispatchers. If you make a habit to go on and off duty with radio dispatch every time, you'll show dispatchers that you are reliable and dependable. This can be important in case you cannot, for some reason, use your radio to request assistance. The dispatcher will realize that something's gone seriously wrong and will begin a search for you when you fail to report. If you have bad radio habits, it may take awhile before anyone worries about you.

Working With a Partner

There are two pieces of advice for two-man patrols: plan ahead and communicate. It's best if you and your partner decide in advance what roles you'll perform and what communications you'll use.

The primary roles are contact officer and security. One partner makes the public contact, while the other officer handles the patrol watercraft and maintains a constant watch for hazards, such as weapons, approaching boats, or obstacles.

When working with a partner, you should switch roles often to avoid becoming stale. You should decide on your roles and tactics before entering a situation and not have to improvise during a crisis. Almost all watercraft patrol officers enjoy operating the watercraft. One rotation switch that works well is for the contact officer to determine what contact to make. After the contact, you reverse roles. This allows the other officer to operate the watercraft. Using a rotation system lets both partners to be equally skilled in all operations, from detecting a violation to seamanship.

Prior communication is extremely important. You must be able to tell your partner that something isn't right without alerting the suspect, for example. It's important to discuss this ahead of time.

There is an excellent handout prepared by Officer Donald L. Holland, of the Garden Grove, California, Police Department, titled "The Garden Grove Hand Signal Method." Its purpose is to provide the officer with an effective but simple means of nonverbal communication. By using verbal communications only, officers cannot control who (them or the subject) will initiate action.

This system can provide you with the ability to communicate in a totally nonverbal form. It consists of 34 different hand signals all basic to understand. For instance, "hostage" is demonstrated by grabbing your neck with one hand as if being choked. "Shotgun" is indicated by simulation of operating a pump shotgun. "Armed" or "gun" is displayed by forming the hand into the shape of a pistol. Other simple hand signals have been developed by other officer teams. Four fingers raised indicates "Code Four," everything is all right, whereas two fingers indicates "Code Two" help. One officer slaps the back of his leg when he's on shore and wants help quickly.

Regardless of what type system is used, it is important for officers to have a clearly understood nonverbal method of communication. There are many occasions when partners become separated by distance and when radios may not be the best way to communicate.

Verbal cues are also necessary. Jerry Scott, of the Ohio Division of Wildlife, points out that his agency uses the four color codes, whereas "code red" indicates a danger warning. Another officer, seeing firearms, would say; "That's a nice pistol you have in your tackle box. What type is it?" This served to alert the partner to the gun and provide for a relaxed conversation. The absolutely worst mistake you can make is to think that your partner is aware of the situation or item. Assumptions can get you seriously hurt.

Regarding planning ahead, partners should discuss different situations that may occur ahead of time. How will you make a felony arrest? If you encounter felons, which of you provides security and who searches and cuffs? It's too easy to ignore simple items, such as where the riot gun is kept, how it is loaded, how it is set up. These can become critical when they are urgently needed. We recommend that whenever you get a new partner, you take 15 minutes to show him where you have all your gear stowed. In a crisis, you can lose valuable minutes while he looks for your first-aid kit or fire extinguisher.

A good way to accomplish this is for your team to informally generate a list of situations you're likely to encounter. From this list, you should prepare some "standard operating procedures." These will more than pay for themselves during a crisis. Take the time to communicate and plan. It's worth it.

One of the best ways to develop good team skills is to allow partners who work together to train together. This doesn't happen often, but if two officers attend the same training classes together and participate in the exercises as a team, their confidence and understanding of each other is enhanced. When working with a partner, to be truly effective, each must learn to anticipate what the other is thinking and what they are going to do. There is no better way to affect this relationship than through training.

If for some reason you are paired with an officer who has a poor survival attitude or is undependable, do whatever you can to get rid of him. There is no "code of honor" where incompetence is concerned. Don't be afraid to go to your supervisor and get him transferred. The "good ol' boys" may not like it, but you're the one who wants to go home in one piece. If you don't stick up for your own safety, no one else will either.

Chapter 8

SHORELINE CONTACTS

Operation and Use of Equipment

Watercraft officers have many occasions to check suspects on shore. You may need to make public contacts to check out violations of various sorts, such as indecent exposure, juvenile alcohol consumption, fireworks (where illegal), firearms, and littering. You'll need to provide public assists and carry out the traditional fisherman bank checks.

Figure 1. Shoreline contacts are frequent during watercraft patrol. Illegal hunting, angling and public safety violations on the water's edge are visible from the water, and officers go ashore to investigate.

Poor seamanship while making shoreline contacts is often a source of embarrassment for the operator and may also cause extensive and expensive engine and hull damage. More importantly, it exposes you and your partner to danger. Regarding seamanship, we have a saying in Region

45

Figure 2. Traditional fisherman bank checks are an important part of many watercraft patrols. The partner controlling the watercraft supports the officer ashore. Rocky banks make beaching the patrol boat almost impossible.

VI, of the Arizona Game and Fish Department: "Experience is directly proportional to the amount of equipment ruined."

You should pick an appropriate place to land, preferably to one side of your contact. Watching for fishing lines and stringers will help avoid fouling your prop or damaging fishing gear. It's good tactics to avoid beaching in the middle of a group, as this makes it harder to keep all subjects under observation. Landing to one side helps you keep everyone in view.

When moving from the relative safety of deep water to the more hazardous shallow water near shore, you must be constantly alert for underwater obstructions. Your patrol craft's speed is important to maintaining control. If speed is too high, you won't have enough time to react to a hazard, but if it's too slow you may lose steerage and be at the mercy of the wind, current or waves.

In the Western United States, where most lakes are formed from dammed rivers, there are usually large underwater rocks near shore. Watch for changes in the water's surface color, which can disclose a rock just under the surface. Approaching shore, you should always trim your engine up as much as possible. Obviously, this applies only to inboard/outboards and outboards. Jet drives require different handling. However,

Figure 3. When near shore, watch out for obstacles which may damage your boat or cause a public complaint. Disembarking to the side away from your subject often avoids these problems.

you don't want to raise the engine so far that you reduce water intake from your engine cooling system.

Leaving the engine down in the water risks breaking props and skegs. You may also suck dirt into the impeller or damage the lower unit. Another consideration is that a trimmed-up engine has a better chance of "skipping" over an obstacle than one trimmed fully down. The real danger to the engine is when you're backing up, as there is no "give" to the engine from a rear blow.

Another danger is wind. Try to maneuver your watercraft to allow the wind to assist your approach, if possible. Waves cause additional problems. The most irritating and dangerous one is when a wave lifts your craft up and over an obstruction, only to leave you stranded on top of it. These are several reasons to time your approach to shore to take advantage of the wave action.

In many cases, when working near rocky shorelines, your best tactic is to approach close enough to allow your partner to jump ashore from the boat's bow. With your partner ashore, you back away quickly but remain close enough to observe events and to help if necessary. If your partner's in danger and needs immediate help, you may have to ram your boat up onto the shore, regardless of possible damage. Your priority is your partner and not your hull.

Figure 4. It's often best to let your partner off on shore to conduct an inspection or write a citation while you provide a watchful eye from the boat on the water. This is especially true where it's impossible to beach the patrol craft.

Beach approaches are similar to shoreline approaches, but the bottom is less hostile to the hull. Applying a little power upon contact with the bottom should provide a secure resting spot. On beaches, it's usually safe to leave the vessel in place while making contacts.

Another major problem occurring during shoreline contacts and general watercraft handling is current. Shoreline approaches on rivers and streams usually require a two-man unit because there are two functions. One is the delicate task of operating into the current, and the other is keeping lookout for underwater obstacles. To retain control, you may trim your engine up, but you must maintain positive steerageway. Once you and your partner have decided the disembarking point, you approach it from downstream, turning the boat into shore, and allowing the current to move your bow downstream. As the bow passes the jump-off point, you give a little power to stabilize the boat and allow your partner to jump to shore. You then reverse and back out, but keep your bow into the current. You can maintain station by using the engine to move against the current. Again, if your partner needs backup, you'll immediately beach the craft, under power and regardless of hull damage.

Trees and brush also pose hazards during shoreline operations. Pick the best location you can find that's free of hazards.

The bottom line is that sometimes a safe shoreline approach isn't possible. You then have to balance your need to go ashore against safety.

One-Officer Watercraft Security

Often, while working one-man patrol, you'll have to leave your watercraft for a shoreline contact. It's wise to carry a portable radio and a baton ashore with you. Some prefer a side-handle baton, but a very convenient one is the the ASP collapsible baton, worn in a belt scabbard.

You need to concern yourself with the security of your watercraft while you are away from it, as violators sometimes steal gear, pull bilge plugs, or even set the boat adrift. Some officers, returning to where they had left their patrol boat, have been embarrassed to discover that it had drifted away.

After you've beached your boat but before you leave it, turn off the electricity and remove the keys. One good technique is to fit a snap to your bow line, which you then hook to your anchor line. This allows you to carry your anchor ashore, tighten the line and then step on the anchor. This way you avoid looking for a suitable tie-down to a rock or bush. If your watercraft has a rubber compression-fit bilge plug, it's more secure to replace it with a brass threaded plug, which can only be removed with a wrench.

You also have to secure removable items in your boat. If you carry a riot gun or rifle, you must have some mechanism to secure it. A lock prevents a curious bystander, perhaps a juvenile, from handling the firearm and possibly causing an accidental discharge.

When you return to your boat, you should carry out a quick security check to ensure that all gear is present and that the boat is functional. This will reveal if anyone has damaged or sabotaged your boat or stolen any gear. Never put a boat onto the water without a safety check if you have left it unattended.

Two-Officer Watercraft Security

Security of a two-man patrol boat is much easier. One officer maintains security, watching both the boat and his partner, while the other makes the contact. If one officer goes ashore, he can hold the bow line. If the security officer leaves the boat for any reason, he must follow the one-officer security routine.

The security officer, if he stays with the boat, also has the choice of casting off and keeping the patrol boat near shore, within easy reach of his partner. This technique is useful when conducting shoreline contacts in current, rough weather, on rocky shorelines, or if the on-shore partner is walking along the shoreline checking fisherman. This allows the on-shore officer and the water officer to coordinate closely, with the officer afloat providing security for his partner.

Communication between both officers is important. They may communicate verbally or use portable radios and hand signals if out of hearing. The water-borne officer must be prepared to issue warnings, beach his boat, or support his partner ashore with gunfire. The officer on the water must never allow himself to become so distracted by other violations that he fails to provide security. He must never leave his partner on the shore while he contacts another violator out of sight of his partner.

It's easy to see that close coordination between partners is vital for their safety. Both must remain alert, not only to their needs, but to their partner's safety. Building this type of cooperation takes time and effort from both officers. Not all are willing. Some may abandon their partners ashore while they pursue another task, showing a serious breach of officer survival practice, and denoting a person who cannot be trusted as a partner.

Chapter 9

CAMPGROUNDS AND LARGE GROUPS

Often, subjects recreating on or near the water won't carry identification with them, especially when dressed only in bathing suits. When you query them for identification, they'll tell you that they left it in their camp or vehicle. Because good identification is essential for issuing a citation in lieu of an arrest, you must obtain identification. Whatever you do, avoid going into a camp or into the middle of a group with a subject to obtain his identification. An incident on the Colorado River showed what can happen when officers allow themselves to be lured too close to a large disorderly group:

During the early 1970s, officers of the Arizona Game and Fish Department were assigned to a strike force to work the Colorado River at Parker, Arizona. At this time, the "Parker Strip" was the site of mass influxes of California college students during spring break. All agencies with jurisdiction in that area sent extra officers to work on the strike force. As the state's primary watercraft patrol, six to eight Arizona Game and Fish officers, working three to four patrol boats, were always assigned.

In one situation, officers stopped a subject for a watercraft violation. He had no identification with him and the officers chose to follow his vessel to shore, where he was camped in a large campground. The crowd ashore converged around the two officers and their patrol boat after they disembarked. An inherent sense of lawlessness, aggravated by use of drugs and alcohol, affected the group's attitude towards "the establishment." Hostile campers surrounded the officers and prevented them from completing their task or returning to their boat. It was necessary to send a team of riot control officers to extract them from the crowd.

In another incident, officers took a subject aboard their patrol watercraft and escorted him to a campground. Upon nearing the camp, a barrage of rocks, beer cans and other thrown debris greeted the boat, and approach to shore was impossible.

This is why we counsel caution when approaching large groups. The officer survival tactics we developed to solve the problems that occurred on these patrols form the basis for this section.

We found that a better technique is to have the suspect board your patrol boat and ask the subject's friends to obtain the documentation for him. During the wait you can fill out the citation, explaining to the subject that any variations between what he tells you and in what his identification states will be grounds for an arrest. This usually persuades him to be truthful. You'll also have time to query for a driver's license and radio confirmation that he has a valid driver's license with matching physical description.

If you stop a subject and ask for identification, it's best to place him on your boat and let his friends go to camp to obtain the paperwork. If you receive a complaint and need to approach a large group, it's better to have the complainant or subject come to you rather than to get into the middle of a large group. Sometimes, you will be fortunate to have undercover officers working the groups. A little coordination will enable you to work the group with "friendlies" for support. Becoming surrounded by potentially hostile people is simply bad tactics.

If you must deal with a large group, single out the apparent leader and address him. Make sure he understands that you will hold him personally responsible for the behavior of the other members. This will help dispel his feelings of group support or anonymity and will establish accountability for his or the group's actions.

Some situations involving large groups can deteriorate very quickly. In such cases, the best move is a strategic withdrawal to safety and calling for backup. Always remember: don't continue with any action if you can't control the outcome. It's better to return with reinforcements later and solve the problem decisively.

There are many factors which cause a large camp or group to be a highly dangerous situation. One reason is that, in a large group, people feel safer than when they're alone. They feel protected by others, which gives them more courage to act. They also take advantage of the fact that you don't know who they are. They know that you'll have difficulty establishing identification later. This perceived anonymity leads to a feeling that no one is accountable and that no one will be personally blamed.

Group cohesiveness is also important. Large groups of people with similar interests and desires, such as juveniles, are more dangerous and more apt to be drawn into crowd hysteria than camps of diversified people or groups of strangers.

Subjects who are usually meek in the presence of officers can turn into aggressive jerks when supported by peers. Support and encouragement

Figure 1. Approach large campgrounds with caution. They contain many dangers to the patrol officer, because an assortment of easily hidden weapons may be available. Another concern is that large unruly groups are impossible to control and may turn on the officers.

by friends can immediately escalate a situation into a crisis. This is why isolating the subject should be the officer's first priority.

Another problem officers face in outdoor campgrounds is the availability of weapons, from knives to firearms. Tents and vehicles provide many places where a suspect may procure dangerous implements or deadly weapons unobserved by an officer.

A suspect may use the crowd as a convenient means to provide escape. Darting into a hostile group will effectively keep you from catching him. Crowds may also attempt to rescue your prisoner by physically taking him from you.

The biggest problem with going into the middle of a crowd is that you cannot control the situation. It can easily get out of hand and turn into a dangerous riot with you as the catalyst and focal point. Another problem is that, in a crowd, it's almost impossible to obtain information about the violation or gather evidence because it's not a controlled scene.

All of the above problems are accentuated by the presence and abuse of drugs and alcohol.

Chapter 10

WATER STOPS

Slow-Speed Approaches

When approaching a boat operating at slow speed or stopped, you should scrutinize it carefully before making contact. A long, slow look before closing in gives you an opportunity to look at the boat's registration numbers and decal and its operating condition. A slow, cautious approach also gives you the time to observe the occupants. You can study their reactions to your approach and decide whether they appear intoxicated, hostile, or furtive. Careful scrutiny allows you to see if any occupants are "stashing" anything.

It's advisable to look the boat over with binoculars before beginning your approach. This shows you who is operating the boat, a crucial point if you're considering issuing a citation regarding the boat's operation. If you're doing fish enforcement, it enables you to see who is fishing. You may also detect other violations, such as illegal drug use or alcohol consumption.

As the subjects become aware of your presence, they may attempt to hide violations or change the situation so as to confuse you. Observation through binoculars will provide you with "probable cause" regardless of any evasive action upon your approach. As there is safety in distance, you can use binoculars to plan ahead instead of making an immediate and direct physical approach. Remember to communicate your knowledge to your partner.

In making your approach, use the best tactics the situation allows. Take full advantage of the elements and the situation. For example, approaching with the rising or setting sun at your back places the subjects at a tactical disadvantage with the sun's rays in their eyes.

When within hailing distance you should identify your agency and your purpose. Maintaining silence until you come alongside increases the subjects' apprehension and may create a hostile contact. A friendly salutation, even when approaching for a violation, will tend to reduce the tension. "Good morning, XYZ Department, we are going to come

Figure 1. Before coming alongside, you should check out the subject boat for number of occupants, possible violations, furtive movements, and any other suspicious activity. Distance provides some safety and using binoculars enhances your survivability.

alongside to do a boating safety inspection," tells the other boaters who you are and what you are doing in a forthright manner without creating undue anxiety. Wearing a visible and well-kept uniform provides immediate recognition and establishes authority. Upon hailing, you should also activate your blue light. With slow-speed contacts in calm water, it may be better to hail without using your public-address system. This lower-profile contact tends to reduce the tension of the approach.

The watercraft patrol officer should always keep in mind that a patrol boat with uniformed officers, blue lights, and a public-address system is very formal and imposing. If you need to be formal, as during a felony arrest, the uniform, lights and sirens are very powerful psychological tools. But when performing basic boating safety checks, they may be too formal for the situation. Over-accentuating these may cause people to resent your approach and presence. This only serves to make your task much harder.

The decision to make your contact from the bow or the side depends upon your agency procedures, water conditions, number of watercraft officers, and your preference. Usually, when on calm waters with a two-man patrol, the bow-on approach is acceptable. Contact over the vessel's sides is preferable for a long-term contact or if you plan to secure the boats together.

The choice of approach from your port or starboard side may be dependent upon environmental conditions, but if you have a two-man patrol boat with an offset helm, the approach should be on the side away from the helm of the patrol boat. Very importantly, the approach should be on the side away from the officer's sidearm. With a one-officer patrol, you may have no choice. You should use the side which provides the best control. You do, however, have several options for boarding, and the best one will be that which keeps your sidearm away from the subjects. You may place your vessel operator to operator, contact officer to operator, or operators apart. The choice will depend on circumstances and you should decide this with your partner, if you have one, before the approach.

Before coming alongside, remember to deploy your fenders or bumpers. Using these buffers properly will reduce damage to the other boat. The contact officer should deploy these well before the hulls touch.

In a congested waterway, it's advisable to use your emergency light. However, in some circumstances it may not be necessary. Agency policies may dictate its use, but on a non-violation safety check, it increases the formality and citizen "embarrassment" of the contact.

Upon coming alongside, you may decide to tie the boats together. If that is standard agency operational procedure, your boat should be rigged with the appropriate lines for this. Holding boats together by hand is tiring and is dangerous in rough water. It also divides your attention and can cause you to lose control of the situation. If the situation requires an extended contact, you should consider tying the boats together.

"Shot bags" are useful tools that speed up securing boats by reducing fumbling for lines and cleats. They also help avoid diverting your attention from the subjects. "Shot bags" are made from the bags in which 25 pounds of lead bird shot are sold. One shot bag, filled with sand and tied to a suitable length of line (and fastened to your cleat), can be dropped into the subject's boat. Two of these weighted lines, from the fore and aft cleats, will hold the boats together in calm to mild waters. Although this technique won't work well with larger boats or heavy waves, it's practical for most pleasure boat contacts and extremely helpful in felony boardings.

Regardless of docking techniques, both officers should be constantly alert for hazards. These may be fishing lines, anchor lines, stringers, or fish baskets. Officers should also watch the subjects' actions, as well as environmental factors such as underwater obstacles, shore or water conditions, and other boating traffic.

Often, the subjects may try to help by reaching for your boat with arms or legs. You should advise them of the dangers and warn them to move their appendages out of the way. If there are children on the other boat, be especially watchful, as they tend to underestimate the dangers. Feet, hands, legs and fingers are especially vulnerable during docking activities. A citizen injury can tie up your day with paperwork and apologies.

Some agencies have equipped patrol boats with trolling motors, which are very useful when performing a large number of fisherman or boating safety checks. Trolling motors allow precise operation while coming alongside, as well as allowing the officer to keep both hands free.

During the approach, some boaters try to help by approaching you. If this happens, you should ask them to shut down and allow you to come alongside. You should also ask them to take in any lines they may have in the water. Depending on shoreline location, wind or other obstacles, you may ask them to move to a different part of the water before you come alongside.

One officer should make the contact and do all the talking and inspecting, while the other officer handles the boat and provides tactical backup. The backup officer should also handle all the radio traffic. Before the contact officer boards the other boat, both officers should have a plan of action to cope with possible problems.

One of the most irritating officer safety problems comes with dogs aboard the subject's boat. Many dogs treat the boat with the same protectiveness they do their master's house. Such dogs will gladly take a chunk out of you when you reach over to grab their gunnel or lean down to secure a line. If there is a dog in the subject's vessel, ask the operator to secure it before you come alongside.

Do you cut your engine or not? This decision may be covered by your agency's procedure, but tactically, it's better to keep your engine running. The reason is that you need to keep your boat under full control, so that you can respond immediately if the situation deteriorates. You may encounter a sudden hazard, such as a strong wind, or waves from other boats. You also may need to take countermeasures or evasive action in case the suspects assault you. Only in rare circumstances may it be advisable to turn off your engine.

If citations are appropriate, the contact officer should write them, following established procedures. If the boat's operator or passengers are giving you a lot of verbal abuse or if you wish to run warrant checks without being overheard, it's advisable to cast off to complete your paperwork and then reestablish contact for the signature. Make sure that you keep your subject's I.D. with you when you do this, to forestall his withdrawing and forcing you into a chase.

The other technique is to have the cited party board your boat. You then cast off to complete your business. This technique isolates the subject from his companions and gives you fewer people to watch. Apart from his companions, the subject will probably be more subdued and easier to handle.

In like manner, if a misdemeanor warrant "hit" occurs, you should have the subject board your watercraft so that you may cast off before you make the arrest. Make sure, however, that anyone remaining on board the other boat can operate it. If not, you may have to tow it. If circumstances permit, you may have the operator drive his boat to shore before you arrest him. Felony arrests require different tactics and we'll cover them later.

During any public contact, you should never accept an invitation to shake hands with a member of the public at any time during the contact. Some people have used this as a ploy to pull the officer off balance. If you are right handed, it ties up your gun hand and impedes effective countermeasures to an assault.

Under normal circumstances, the contact officer should leave with an appropriate closing remark that ends the contact on a positive note. The contact officer should also watch the other boat during departure to provide officer security and also observe any activities on-board.

High-Speed Approaches

High-speed approaches are those made to boats on plane, when it's necessary to pursue the other vessel, overtake it and have the operator shut down so you can board. Officers initiate these when observing a violation or when there's reasonable suspicion that a violation is occurring.

When you initiate a high-speed approach, you should always turn on your blue light. You may use the siren, if necessary, to warn other boaters or to attract the subject's attention.

When in pursuit, never follow directly behind the boat in his wake. Remain to the port or starboard side. This is because some suspects have been known to throw debris overboard to damage the pursuing patrol boat. Remaining off to the side allows you to get out of his wake, gives you room to maneuver, and allows you to overtake him with minimal danger. An important point to watch is to be careful if near shore. Do not attempt to overtake with your boat between the other boat and the shoreline. This leaves you with restricted maneuvering room, especially around "points." At worst, if he makes an inside turn, he may drive you upon the rocks.

Figure 2. When performing high-speed pursuits, never follow directly astern the suspect boat. Remaining on the port or starboard side while overtaking provides you with room to maneuver and may help prevent collision if the suspect makes a quick turn.

During a high-speed approach, the contact officer must always observe the subject vessel and keep the operating officer informed. Once you have the subject operator's attention, you can signal for him to stop or hail him with your P.A. Most subjects will stop immediately upon command. This shows another good reason for not pursuing from directly astern. Some subjects, however, will panic and turn their boats. You have to avoid collision and remain watchful for other traffic, as well as for irregularities in operation of the pursued vessel.

Figure 3. Do not pursue between the suspect boat and the shoreline. Give yourself plenty of room for evasive action.

If the subject decides to flee, you should use your siren and pursue as described above. Stopping a fleeing boat is very difficult and there appear to only be two techniques for doing this. One is to chase him until he runs out of water or fuel, providing your boat is fast enough to keep up with him. The other is to foul his propeller. This is a dangerous operation and is usually only suitable with a runaway boat that continues to run at high speed in a circle. If you have adequate communications and help on shore, you may have the suspect picked up when he comes off the water. High-speed pursuits are dangerous and you may decide to break off the attempt if it becomes unsafe. If there are other ways to apprehend him, you should utilize those techniques. Get the best description you can and then call for help.

If, on the other hand, the operator follows your instructions and comes to a stop, you then proceed with the slow-speed approach, or felony boarding techniques, depending on the circumstances.

Water-Skier Approaches

Many high-speed approaches involve water-skiers. When approaching a boat towing a water-skier, do not follow in the subject boat's wake, because you need to ensure that you avoid the water-skier. This eliminates the risk that your boat may run over a falling water-skier or that he may be sucked into your prop and seriously injured.

The rest of the approach and stop for a water-skier is the same as a high-speed approach, except that when the subject boat stops dead in the water, order the operator to bring the skier, ski rope and skis aboard the subject vessel before you make your slow-speed approach. If the stop takes place in a busy waterway, you may use the patrol boat to protect the skier until he is out of the water.

When taking the skier onto the patrol boat, always turn off your engine before he boards. Putting it into neutral for a stern boarding can be a very serious accident just waiting to happen. However, if the skier can board your boat away from the stern, you may not need to cut your engine.

Disabled Boats and Request for Assistance Approaches

Disabled boats are quite common, and citizens will often request assistance. The approach to a request for assistance is the same as for a slow-speed approach but with one difference. Do not come alongside until you can identify the nature of the problem. Optimum distance is between 20 and 25 feet. Always ask the occupants what their exact problem is before the final approach. This provides an opportunity for you to observe how they respond to questions and gain an early warning of a possible setup.

You must be on the lookout for problems that your boat may create. If, for example, the disabled boat is taking on water or is seriously overloaded, your boat's wake may swamp them. Another crucial point is never to secure lines to a sinking boat, because you might be swamped. Concentrate your efforts on rescuing the occupants. Safety always comes before equipment.

Another point is to be constantly wary of a setup. Never go into a potentially dangerous situation without having scanned the scene well in advance.

If you need to rescue persons from other vessels, the bow area is the safest. Stern rescues require turning off your engine. Patrol boats should have stern-mounted boarding ladders or dive platforms. These are good for the purpose, but sound safety practice still requires turning off your engine. There are several well-made portable boarding ladders on the market. These allow easy access from swimmers to your boat from the sides and away from your prop. If, for some reason, you have swimmers in the water around your boat, you must be careful not to endanger them with your prop. The best technique is to turn it off as fast as you can. In an emergency, the kill switch is the fastest way to shut down an engine. Another point is that anyone brought on board should wear a PFD.

Whether you elect to tow or jump-start another vessel depends on your evaluation of the situation and your agency's policies and procedures.

Keep in mind that jump-starting is very dangerous and should never be performed battery-to-battery. Your patrol boat should have a remote jumping setup. For the best result, let the other person hook up his battery first. No spark can occur if the other ends of the cables aren't connected to your battery. Once he's connected, have him move away from his battery, then connect the cables to your remote terminals. This prevents sparking near the battery. Hydrogen gas is very explosive and a battery can turn into a bomb. When power is applied to the jumped battery, the boat's occupants should be well away from it. It's best to place a towel or rag over the bad battery before applying power.

Always keep a close eye on the citizen you're helping. During a jump start one night, the citizen struck a lighter near his batteries to see if he'd connected the cables to the right terminals!

A type of installation used on some modern boats is to have the jumper cables hard-wired to the battery but with a double-pole, single-throw switch to keep them deactivated when not in use. When it's necessary to provide a jump start, the officer hands his cables to the operator of the disabled boat, who can connect them to his terminals without fear of danger, because they are not "hot." When they're securely connected, the officer turns on the power to the other boat.

Many officers are reluctant to jump batteries, but the irony is that most jumps I have been involved with were jumps to bad batteries on water-craft patrol boats! Even if agency policy doesn't allow you to jump a public battery, you may end up having to know how to jump yours. The danger is the same.

You should always be careful upon encountering an unattended boat.

You should look over the boat, but never allow your attention to be so absorbed by it that you are unaware of its occupants and their activity. You should be aware of the potential for booby traps, which we'll discuss later.

Chapter 11

INSPECTIONS

One of the most frequent duties a watercraft patrol officer performs is the boating safety inspection. This inspection begins after stopping and approaching the subject boat. When starting an inspection, remember that the subject's attitude and degree of cooperativeness may reveal a potential problem. Remember, however, that professional criminals will probably give you no clue that they're involved in illegal activities.

Keep in mind that some subjects may try to "short circuit" your inspection by distracting you from your objective. If the boat and equipment appear to be in order and the operator or others in the boat are behaving in a manner that is not appropriate, they may be trying to keep you from discovering something they are hiding. This may range from insufficient PFDs to dope. When faced with this situation, you must retain control, but their actions should make you more cautious and more determined to complete your task. Don't be intimidated or deterred from completing your inspection by verbal hostility. One way to handle such a situation is to use a technique mentioned earlier: that of singling out the leader and making him personally responsible for the group's behavior and any consequences.

There are many tricks violators may use to keep you from finding their "secrets" and inappropriate hostility is only one of them. Ask yourself "why are these people acting that way?" and stick to your task.

As described earlier, one of you should make the inspection while the other officer handles the patrol boat and provides security. If for some reason, you must physically board the subject's vessel, you should have worked out a communication plan with your partner to alert him to danger and to coordinate your actions.

There are several articles in the police literature describing problems that have occurred when officers became separated during boarding incidents. In the Winter 1988–1989 issue of *International Game Warden* magazine, an article titled "Thrown Overboard to Die!" graphically illustrates this point:

Figure 1. When inspecting a boat, keep a sharp eye on the subject. His behavior can provide a cue regarding a serious problem.

Two state officers and a federal warden were checking on the illegal use of gill nets on Lake Superior. A Canadian vessel operating in U.S. waters was boarded by one of the state officers. A fight ensued and, during the scuffle, a suspect threw the state officer overboard into 39-degree water. The Canadian vessel then made a run for Canadian waters. The state boat, too slow to catch the suspect's boat, rescued the officer just before the officer was overcome with hypothermia. Although this is a quick summary of the actual event, it shows that boardings have the potential for danger and that the Five Deadly Sins and their cure do apply.

When you come alongside for your inspection, one of the first things you should do (this assumes that you have completed all of the steps stated in the slow-speed approach section, i.e. statement of identification and purpose, fenders out, subject boat's engine turned off, and boats secured) is obtain the registration papers and operator's identification. The acquisition of his personal paperwork is one of the first steps in exerting control. The reason is that people are very dependent on paperwork. Once you possess someone's ID, psychologically, you now possess him. He is no longer an unknown. Assuming your subject is not providing a false ID, you now know who he is and where he lives. A subject is less likely to fight or flee when he knows you can locate him later. Once you've got his ID and registration, you should go through the inspection itself, not returning his ID until you're finished.

It's helpful to develop a routine for your inspections. If your routine is based on good watercraft patrol inspection techniques and officer tactics, it will help you maintain track of where you are and what you're seeking. You're also less likely to forget something if distracted.

If you need to run any registrations, HINs or warrant checks and are working two-man patrol, pass the paperwork to your partner on the patrol boat. As we've emphasized throughout, you and your partner need to have a routine and a system worked out to communicate the results of your radio check. If, for example, your partner is five feet from the suspect and there's a felony warrant "hit," you need to be able to convey to your partner that the person is wanted without alerting the suspect or losing control.

One tactic is to cast off from the subject boat with your partner while you perform radio checks, withdrawing far enough to prevent the subject from hearing radio traffic. The reason is that, in some open patrol boats, the subject can hear the radio quite clearly. If a warrant or stolen boat hit comes back and he hears it the same time as you, you have lost the advantages of surprise and prior planning and the initiative passes to him.

As state laws vary regarding equipment and registration requirements, there's no point in going deeply into the details of a proper boating inspection. There are also so many combinations of events that it's impossible to present tactics for all of them. The main points are to communicate, plan ahead, maintain control, and not be distracted from your purpose.

During your inspection, it may be advisable to order the subject boat off the water to correct safety problems. If you have to do this, be polite, but firm, and provide an explanation of why it must be done. You should, of course, retain the operator's ID and registration until he is safely ashore. You should also specify the landing point, to avoid his leading you into the middle of a hostile camp.

Another point to consider during inspections is that an officer is exposing himself to a serious liability if his inspection uncovers a safety violation and he does not take sufficient steps to correct it. Once you contact a boat, you assume responsibility, especially if you uncover an unsafe condition.

If the subject's boat is overloaded, it may be necessary to take surplus passengers aboard your boat while you escort the other vessel to shore. If you encounter such a situation, make sure that your boat does not exceed its carrying capacity and that all passengers have safe seating and are wearing PFDs.

If they have too few PFD's, you'll have to lend them some until you've escorted them to shore. You'll also have to handle other safety problems in like manner, to protect the public and yourself.

An important point is to issue a citation or complaint of violation when ordering a boat off the water. A verbal warning (usually defined as a "break") is indefensible if a citizen makes a complaint against you for "harassment." At that time it's your word against his that you had probable cause to order him off the water. You'll be spending your time defending your actions against a harassment charge and explaining why you ruined his family's weekend. A citation backs up the legal reasons for your actions.

This opinion is expressed quite well by some experienced officers as, "No good deed will ever remain unpunished." Some people consider a verbal warning as a "lecture" and become more upset with that than with a ticket. This type of complaint is common after a busy weekend.

Occasionally, you'll need to seize a boat. During inspections, this would usually occur if you have reason to believe the boat is stolen or if it's transporting contraband. Another (non-felonious) reason is if the operator is disabled or if nobody aboard is able to operate the boat. It is a lot easier to seize a boat on its trailer than on the water. You need to plan ahead and think out the best way for you to handle this situation. A good tactic is to get the boat to shore before you seize it. This eliminates part of the responsibility for the boat's passengers, or how to get it out of the water. When ordering a boat to shore for this purpose, don't tell the subject that you're about to seize his boat until you have the situation under firm control. This prevents the operator or his friends working out a plan of action while you're escorting them to shore.

Chapter 12

STOLEN BOATS

Watercraft officers will often encounter stolen boats. What happens next depends on whether you recognize the boat as stolen. You may be on patrol and have several stolen boats pass you without any obvious sign that they're not legitimate. You may be conducting a routine safety inspection and be unaware that the boat's operator is not the legitimate owner. Worse, you may become aware that something is wrong too late, after you've placed yourself in a position where you're vulnerable.

Figure 1. Stolen boats come in all shapes and sizes. Jet skis are popular items to steal, rework, and resell.

On the water, as well as on land, it's important for the officer to learn as much as he can about a situation before approaching. For your safety, you need to work your way in methodically, not taking the next step until you've checked out what you can from a distance.

This is why it's valuable to know and understand some early warning signals that signify that a boat may be stolen. Some are apparent from a distance, alerting you before you approach. Others show themselves upon closer inspection. Let's begin with what you can see from afar.

First, how big is the boat? Boat theft is mainly a small boat problem. Eighty percent of stolen boats are under 22 feet in length.

The environment and operating conditions may provide the first alert. A boat which doesn't seem to fit in with its surroundings alerts you that something may be wrong. An expensive pleasure cruiser in an economically depressed area is out of place and raises the question regarding why its operator would be in that particular location. This warrants a closer look before approaching. So does a boat operating at night without lights. This may be a simple violation or an attempt to avoid drawing attention to a stolen boat.

Some environments are favorable for people trying to dispose of stolen boats and, if they have the cooperation of the proprietors, may actually be "boat-laundering" operations. Marinas with large storage areas are good for warehousing stolen boats prior to disposal. Any boat storage area in a locale where there have been many thefts is worth a careful look. Boatyards with many used boats for sale are worth a systematic inspection, because a few stolen boats may be among the inventory.

A boat matching the description of a stolen boat is an obvious sign. A look at the operator and passengers may reveal that they are known criminals or suspects. An abandoned boat may have been taken for a joyride.

A pair of binoculars often helps, letting you see details that otherwise would be obscure until you got too close for safety. Check for registration numbers on the hull. Regulations specify location and size of characters. If there are no registration numbers and the boat is not brand new, it's cause for investigation.

Binoculars also help scrutinize the way numbers are marked. Evidence of new numbers painted over old ones suggests something irregular. So does lack of a manufacturer's name on the boat, or signs that the name's been covered or repainted. If the area around the numbers shows signs of having been cleaned or buffed, it's important to find the reason why.

It may be possible to scrutinize the boat's paint job from a distance. A fairly new boat which appears to have just had another paint job is suspect.

Some indications of tampering show up only after pulling alongside and beginning the inspection. The first step is inspecting the registration and comparing it with the boat's description and HIN. If these don't match you have a red flag. Sometimes, only close inspection will reveal obliterated or changed numbers.

The registration may have signs which, although not conclusive by themselves, are suggestions for further investigation. A registration in a county or state far from the area of operation may be suspicious, unless it's normal for boaters to travel from afar to use that particular waterway. Registration numbers inconsistent with the boat's apparent age also suggests an irregularity. A certificate that lists the boat as "homemade" or "custom built" may be a ploy to disguise its origin. A previous out-of-state registration, or one from another country, also suggests the need for further checking.

Only if the boat appears impeccable up to this point should you consider boarding. Once aboard the other boat, you're literally within touching distance of the operator and his passengers. If they're truly suspects, you're in danger.

Boarding the boat lets you see details close up. Some modifications, such as altering the HIN, are illegal. While checking the engine, you may notice that the motor number shows signs of tampering. This suggests that you need to back off and go over the registration and HIN again, possibly inviting the operator to the dock for a detailed inspection. Look for serial numbers of other equipment, which may reveal stolen "hits." Items such as depth finders, trolling motors, and radios often carry serial numbers.

The main point is, if you notice anything irregular while aboard the suspect boat, don't announce it. For your own safety, make your way back aboard your boat before taking appropriate tactical action.

Chapter 13

ARRESTS

Pursuits

As mentioned earlier with high-speed approaches, pursuits on the water are occasionally necessary. You should remember that there is a burden of liability on your shoulders when you are in pursuit. This is why you should take every precaution to protect the safety of the public. Operate your lights and siren, keep your dispatcher advised, and remember not to follow astern. Do not violate any standards of good seamanship and don't take any unnecessary risks.

Younger and less experienced officers sometimes are "hot dogs" and have too much enthusiasm for the chase, to the point of taking needless

Figure 1. When pursuing a suspect, remember that you may be liable for any accidents or damage that may occur as a result. Depending on local laws, lights and siren should be on and you should avoid unnecessary risks to yourself or to the public.

risks. When deciding to pursue, always keep in mind that if you're injured or your boat is disabled, you can't do your job. Someone else will have to rescue you. Always balance the risks of the pursuit against the risks to the public of allowing the other boat to escape.

While you are in pursuit, decide with your partner on your roles at the stop. If you've worked together before, you'll probably have already planned for similar incidents and won't need a detailed discussion.

When approaching a suspect boat that has fled from you, do not be too eager to close and board with the violator. You don't know his reason for flight and it's best to be careful. Stand off about 25 yards and assert control before you approach.

Once you've established control and approach the boat, local laws define the exact nature of the violation. In certain jurisdictions, flight from a peace officer is a felony, while in others it is a misdemeanor. The severity of the offense will dictate your response. Just remember, the suspect may not know, nor care, what the local statutes are, because he obviously had something to hide from you. Treat the situation with extreme caution, and practice good officer survival tactics.

Citation vs. Arrest

If it's necessary to issue a citation, you should retain the subject's identification until after he signs the citation. Do not hand it over to him clipped on your citation book. As we've already seen, retaining the subject's ID maintains a measure of control over him.

Physical arrest is sometimes necessary. This changes the situation drastically, because you are now responsible for the suspect's safety as well as his custody. If the situation permits, you should get your subject onto land before informing him that he's under arrest. A scuffle on the water is very dangerous and can easily result in one or more participants going overboard. A good tactic is to have the suspect take his boat to the marina, launch ramp, or beach, where you wish to make contact. Once his boat is secured, you can move him away from any crowd and make the arrest. Always handcuff first and then search anyone whom you arrest.[1]

Sometimes, it may be impossible to get the suspect to shore before having to arrest him. Making an arrest on the water is hazardous, as we've discussed, but there are ways to lessen the risk. One way is to have him board your boat, move away from the area, and place him under arrest. This is especially important if you are working alone. However, the methods laid out here do not apply to armed and dangerous felons. Other tactics are necessary for a full-scale felony stop. After the arrest, make sure you advise someone from his party what you have done and where he is going to be.

Violator Safety

If possible, obtain the suspect's boat keys before informing him that he's under arrest. This is a psychologically deflating tactic and prevents him from attempting to start his engine and leave.

In case a fight begins, you should pull your kill switch immediately. This will avoid propeller injury if anyone goes overboard. It will also avoid a runaway boat problem.

Often, the only firearm at the scene will be yours. This is why it's very important for you to never expose your sidearm to a suspect. This will deter him from considering a "snatch." Having a tight-fitting holster and well-maintained gun belt will reduce the danger of a successful snatch. If the suspect tries for your holstered sidearm, the best countermove is to clamp the weapon in with your closest hand and turn hard against the suspect's elbow. This will break his grip (and probably his elbow) and place you in a good position to hand-cuff him.

We stress again that it's a good tactic, if the suspect is not alone, to separate him from the rest of his party. Having him board your patrol boat is one way to gain immediate control of his person. However, be sure that he has no access to deadly weapons aboard your boat. You should remain alert to the prospect of anyone else trying to board to reinforce or rescue the suspect. Creating distance between your boat and the other is one way of forestalling this.

Occasionally, a subject will be incapable of operating his watercraft as a result of illness. If it's due to alcohol or drugs and no one else aboard can operate his boat, you must arrest him and then decide what to do with his boat and passengers. This decision may be forced upon you for some other reason, but you are responsible to see that passengers reach shore safely. Your responsibility covers both damage to his boat and the safety of his passengers. You need to avoid any hazardous situations that may occur due to other boat traffic or environment.

You should use appropriate handcuffing techniques. There are many techniques being taught, but you should use the one that you have practiced and with which you're comfortable. Generally, a suspect should kneel before cuffing, as this reduces his center of gravity and may avoid a mishap in rough water. Once he is kneeling, however, his center of gravity is lower than yours. You must be careful and keep in mind that if the suspect decides to butt you with his head or shoulder, he'll have the advantage. Another important point is always to handcuff the suspect's hands behind his back.[2]

During the arrest, resist any temptation to use humor to lighten the incident, because this may create later problems when you get to court. Always be firm, businesslike and understanding.

As in any other arrest, you must search the suspect for weapons. Female suspects must also be searched using techniques designed to disarm the "sexual abuse" charge. One technique is to run a mini-flashlight along the pockets, waist, and clothing seams, to avoid hand-to-body contact. The mini-flashlight will click when contacting a hard object. Another aspect of searching is to avoid harm from a drug user's concealed needles. Some particularly obnoxious suspects have been known to sew razor blades or fish hooks into their clothing to injure police officers searching them. Using a mini-flashlight is a safe way to avoid harm.[3]

Once you arrest a suspect, it's your duty to equip him with a PFD. The Type I is preferable, as this one turns the suspect face up in the water. A prisoner with his hands cuffed behind his back will have difficulty keeping his face out of the water with a Type III. Never place a Type III PFD on a prisoner, because if he falls overboard he may float face down long enough to drown.

The Cooperative Subject

With a cooperative subject, you have much more flexibility in dealing with the situation. You have four basic options:

1. Issue the citation alongside.
2. Issue the citation in your boat "cast off" from the other vessel. (This may be used to separate the subject from trouble-makers on his boat and is very useful when in rough water, as you do not need to be tied alongside. Make sure, however, that someone in his boat can operate it.)

3. Arrest on shore.
4. Arrest on your boat and equip the suspect with a Type I PFD before cuffing.

The Uncooperative Suspect

The uncooperative suspect poses more problems and reduces your flexibility. Keeping control of him, his property and his friends is essential. When he is aboard your boat and you are cast off from his support, tact and diplomacy usually work. When they fail, however, you must use only that force necessary to effect the arrest. Don't play "catchup," however violent he's been. The important point about an arrest is to use only the force necessary to control the suspect, and any excess can work against you in court. Defense attorneys often try for a "brutality" angle if they feel they have a chance, which is why it's smart never to provide them with an opening.

Keeping the suspect under "control" means having him with his hands cuffed behind his back. Once finished with the search, do not release the suspect's hands to put on a Type I PFD. Your only choice is to place a Type II on the prisoner before transportation. A suspect who must be physically subdued in order to arrest him has forfeited the use of a Type I PFD.

Felony Boarding Tactics

Most police academies teach felony vehicle takedown techniques. It seems reasonable that watercraft patrol officers may find themselves in a situation where a felony takedown and boarding of a vessel might occur. Our expectations and training must be geared for this need.

The main fact is that, in felony boarding, there is no safe way for a single officer to safely control the scene. He must wait for backup in order to ensure his own safety.

There are many instances that will require a felony boarding. Typically, these are felonies during which the fleeing felon uses a boat for escape. Another is when suspects use a vessel to transport contraband. In this type of situation, you probably will receive radio traffic concerning the violation. If you are in the area, let the dispatcher know where you are and request complete information regarding the boat and suspect description before you commit yourself.

Captains Mike Tucker and Ken Willoughby, of the Florida Marine Patrol, have developed and are teaching techniques for "high-risk boardings." The following techniques are adapted from those they teach at their academy.

For this discussion, we will assume a two-officer patrol. One officer takes the "contact" role, the other is the "covering" officer. The contact officer's role is to issue verbal challenges and perform the docking, boarding, handcuffing, and searching operations. The cover officer's job is to provide protection to the contact officer by maintaining overall surveillance and control of the suspect(s).

The cover officer must choose his firearm carefully. Each type of firearm, shotgun, sidearm and rifle has its advantages. The most important criterion for selection is the cover officer's confidence in the firearm he chooses.

The cover officer must maintain cover and concealment during the contact, and he must avoid placing the contact officer in front of his muzzle or in a cross fire. In order to successfully accomplish this, he will have to change position as the contact progresses, while providing constant security.

When you're searching for the suspect boat, you and your partner need to decide on roles. You also must prepare equipment necessary for the arrest and place it where it will be readily available. For instance, it's better to look for your Type II PFDs now instead of when you need them!

Upon spotting the suspect vessel, inform your dispatcher of your location and plan. You must select the place to make the stop, preferably away from innocent persons. An important factor in this calculation is that handgun bullets can fly unobstructed for hundreds of yards on the water. Rifle bullets have even greater range. Try to make the stop where you have a clear zone of fire. As you approach the suspect boat, maintain a distance of at least 20–25 yards behind them. At this time, you need to gain the suspects' attention and to make sure they know that they're being stopped by police officers. This is particularly important when using low-profile or unmarked boats, to forestall suspects' later claiming that they thought they were being accosted. The use of the uniform, blue lights, and siren provides you with a psychological advantage. It establishes the basis for your authority and creates a climate favorable for arrest.

During the final approach, the cover officer keeps the suspects covered with his firearm, using cover and concealment. Meanwhile, the contact officer operates the patrol boat and uses the P.A.

At this point, you inform the suspects of your identity as a police officer, using the P.A. for clarity. Identify yourselves as "POLICE," because this is a universal symbol of authority. Titles such as "park ranger," "game warden," "conservation officer," "marine patrol," etc., may be technically correct, but when it's necessary to establish immediate control, "police" leaves no room for misunderstanding.

The contact officer then orders the suspects to turn off their engine and stand by for boarding. He tells them that you are coming alongside and warns them regarding what you are prepared to do if your orders are not obeyed: "We are coming alongside. If you resist you will get hurt. Do you understand?" This type of order accomplishes two purposes. One is that it forestalls the suspects' claim in court that you used force. In reality, you told him what to do and it was his decision to resist by force. Second, they must acknowledge your orders. "Do you understand?" requires feedback from them. When they reply, it establishes that they understand the warning. It also helps establish your control over them.

Once this is completed, the contact officer orders the suspects to turn away from him. He also orders them to stay together. You don't want suspects to separate, because it's more difficult to cover persons spread apart. Remember that stress may cause you and your partner to experience "tunnel vision," and that keeping the suspects together helps to mitigate this.

Once the suspects are facing away from you, order them to place their hands on their heads, with fingers interlaced. Have the suspects move to the side of the boat away from where you are going to board, but don't let them take a position that provides any cover or concealment. You don't want them able to obtain weapons unseen by you or your partner.

At this point, you are still 20 to 25 yards behind their vessel. Don't get any closer until you're sure that they're obeying your orders. It's a serious error to be in a hurry to board. If the cover officer sees any danger, he should warn his partner and correct the situation. If the suspects are submitting, the contact officer moves the boat to the boarding position. He repeats his previous command: "We are going to board. If you resist you will be hurt. Do you understand?" With an acknowledgment, he then pulls the patrol boat into boarding position. Before boarding, he orders the suspects to the kneeling position, keeping faced away and with their fingers interlaced on their heads.

Figure 2. After coming alongside, the cover officer maintains control while the contact officer secures the boats together.

When the scene seems secure, the contact officer draws his sidearm and also covers the suspects as he leaves the helm. He then secures the boats together. An important preparation for boarding is to bring enough handcuffs or nylon restraints to handle all suspects.

Upon boarding, his first act is to look for hidden weapons and other suspects. He approaches the closest suspect and cuffs and searches him. The sequence is always the same: cuff, then search. He repeats this with each suspect. Also, upon initial approach, he should be watchful for any weapons or for hidden suspects.

When the contact officer finishes handcuffing and searching the suspects, he brings them to the patrol boat one at a time, secures a PFD and helps them cross over to the patrol boat.

Each suspect assumes a prone or kneeling position under the watchful eye of the cover officer. The contact officer does this with each suspect until they're all aboard the patrol boat. The cover officer must not allow the contact officer's actions, or those of his prisoner, to distract him from his primary task of keeping control of the other suspects.

The contact officer now boards the suspect boat and performs a thorough check for weapons and hidden suspects. Depending on agency policy, the contact officer prepares the seized boat for towing, operates the patrol boat, and communicates with the dispatcher and other

Figure 3. With the cover officer watching the suspects, the contact officer prepares to board their boat.

Figure 4. The contact officer handcuffs suspects FIRST, while the cover officer maintains security.

Figure 5. Once he has the suspects handcuffed, the contact officer searches each thoroughly.

Figure 6. When searches are completed and all weapons controlled, the contact officer puts a PFD on each suspect before they are transferred to the patrol watercraft.

responding units of their status. Meanwhile, the cover officer maintains prisoner surveillance and security.

Using two single-officer patrol boats is inappropriate for a felony stop. Good tactics suggest that officers abandon one boat and double up before searching. Officers separated on each boat will have a harder time communicating. It takes too much attention to operate a boat and maintain cover. The increased risk is unacceptable.

If you have two patrol boats with two officers each, you must pay special attention to positioning in order to avoid catching each other in a cross fire, which would negate the firepower of each boat. The two boats should deploy in a primary and secondary contact fashion, with the primary boat performing the boarding. The secondary, or backup, patrol boat should maintain a 20-yard distance behind the suspects' boat and provide cover. Never sandwich the felony boat between the patrol boats. It looks neat and symmetrical, but officers can't use their firearms without fear of hitting a fellow officer.

Prisoner Transport and Security

Once arrested and on your boat, the suspect should be past resisting. If the suspect continues to struggle, you must transport him in the prone position. Place a Type IV cushion under his head to prevent injury.

If he still refuses to cooperate you may need to use a security strap to restrain him. Also known as "dog leashes," these are easily constructed from a 3-foot piece of line. Tie a non-closing loop at one end and a snap at the other end. These leashes are also available commercially.

To use it, you place the noose over his feet, bring his legs up, put the line around the cuffs, then snap the line to loop around his feet. Be careful, though. Under no circumstances is it advisable to tie him to any part of the boat.

Some units are equipped with transport belts, but typically these are not for field arrests. They are designed for transportation of prisoners from one controlled place to another.

While transporting, keep the prisoner in a place where he is under constant observation and you can get to him quickly. Keep in mind that handcuffs are only temporary restraints. If the suspect is seated next to you, keep your body between him and your sidearm, even if this means rotating your gun belt 180 degrees.

You must operate your boat in a safe and reasonable manner. Proceed

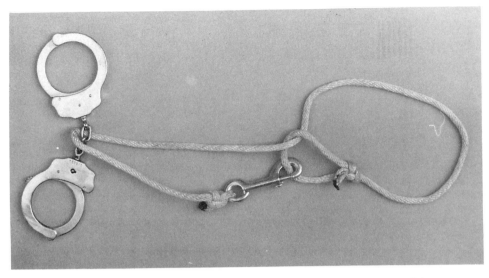

Figure 7. A security strap is an inexpensive device that is invaluable to secure a violent suspect for water transportation. This shows how to attach it to a suspect.

through choppy water or cross wakes at a slow speed. With his hands cuffed behind him, your prisoner will not be able to protect himself from injury.

Whenever possible, have a shore unit meet with you to transport the suspect to the jail facility. Do not put your prisoner on public display, as seclusion maintains your advantage. The prisoner loses a potential audience and the opportunity to show off his courage.

Seizures

Occasionally you will seize a boat because it's carrying contraband or because it is stolen. You may end up towing a non-seized boat because the boat is inoperable or the operator is incapacitated. Another reason is that the boat may be abandoned. When seizing a boat, you must follow your agency policies regarding search and seizure. Many states have seizure inspection forms. As with vehicles, if you routinely inspect seized boats as part of agency procedures, to protect property, items you find will probably be admissible. The best recommendation is to follow agency direction.

Officer survival comes into play when searching inanimate objects, as well. Beware of booby traps and other problems suspects can cause you.

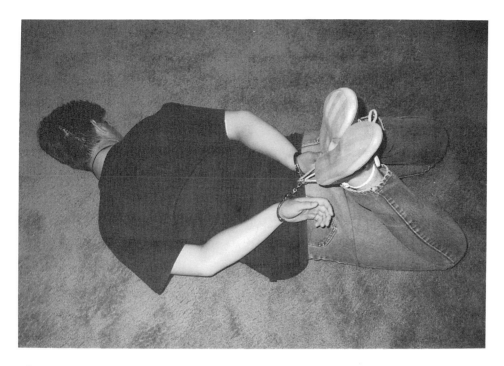

Figure 8. Securely restrained with handcuffs and a security strap, this suspect is ready to travel. Remember to place a cushion under his head, because you're liable if he gets hurt.

Never put your unprotected hand into any place you cannot see. Use a flashlight or mirror to see what's inside first.

Hostile Environments

There may be occasions when it's just too dangerous to take enforcement action. You need to use common sense in relating your actions in the light of local conditions. Always err on the side of personal safety. If you obtain good identification of the subjects, you can afford to bide your time and then take action when conditions are in your favor.

NOTES

1. John G. Peters, Jr., *Tactical Handcuffing*, Albuquerque, New Mexico, 1988, p. 71.
2. Ibid., p. 76.
3. Ibid., p. 90.

Figure 9. Officers will occasionally need to impound a boat. They can be of any size, but if stolen, or if the operator is under the influence, they are candidates for a tow.

Chapter 14

ACCIDENT RESPONSES

While on watercraft patrol, you'll receive calls directing you to respond to a boating accident or accidents. When you take the call, make sure you obtain the exact location of the accident. In some areas this might entail taking LORAN, VOR, or latitude/longitude locations. If you're familiar with your patrol area, you'll find it easier to visualize the location of the accident and select the fastest response route. While in transit, start planning your actions for arrival at the scene.

Transit time can be quite lengthy, unlike conditions on city streets, which gives you plenty of time for planning and preparation. One important preliminary step is to query your dispatcher for additional information, such as the number of boats involved and the nature and extent of injuries. This will help you plan and to decide whether or not you should try to have additional help on the scene. Information already available to the dispatcher may indicate the need for backup officers, an air-evacuation helicopter, or a ground ambulance, if the scene is near vehicle access.

When you arrive at the accident, your duties will include controlling and protecting the scene. First, though, assess the situation. "Size up" the situation, as Steve King, paramedic-firefighter with Palm Beach County, Florida, Fire-Rescue, points out.[1] Making a first estimate allows you to assign priorities and avoid endangering yourself or the victims. What type of first aid do the victims need? Do you need any backup, and what sort? Will you need to call for additional rescue services? Is there an immediate danger of explosions or fire? Are any victims missing? Are any boats in danger of sinking or capsizing? Will you need assistance to control traffic? Do you need other law enforcement backup? Answering these questions will point the way towards solving the problem.

As with road accidents, life takes precedence over property. Protecting life includes providing medical aid for the injured and safeguarding others at the scene from injury. This may include evacuating people from a burning or sinking boat and pulling swimmers out of the water.

Once you take responsibility for these people, make sure that you provide them with PFDs. You should also consider the possibility that one or more victims may have injuries of which they may be unaware. A quick medical assessment may reveal them.

If there are too many people in the water to take them all aboard your boat, quickly throw out some ring buoys or other flotation devices and load them as efficiently as you can. You may be able to ferry some ashore, but you may also have to call for backup to transport all of the victims.

There will be times when you'll have to enter the water to perform first aid or place the victim on a back board. When approaching an accident scene where rescue operations will be necessary, it's wise to store your gun belt in a secure area. In a rescue attempt, you probably won't need it and its weight and bulk can impede your efforts. To allow shedding your gun belt quickly, don't wear "keepers" while on watercraft patrol. A fall overboard may also require shedding excess weight, but keepers hinder this process.

If you do have to enter the water, make sure that you wear a PFD, because very few watercraft patrol officers are certified and practiced lifeguards. If there are victims in the water, you should rescue them with the "Reach, Throw, Row, Go" techniques.

Pike poles or paddles can be used to "Reach." Every patrol watercraft should carry Type IV ring buoys (secured to a line) and/or throw bags. These are very effective and are for the "Throw" option. "Row" means to use a boat to reach the victim. Obviously, you're already using that option. The only time an officer should "Go" into the water to rescue a victim is if the officer is highly trained for swimming rescue techniques or if the victim needs in-water first aid. You want to avoid "double drowning," i.e. in which the rescuer and the victim both drown.

Think hard about going into the water to administer first aid before you commit yourself to it. Weather and water conditions, and the victim's injuries, will be factors to consider.

In one case, during a Memorial Day patrol on Roosevelt Lake, Arizona, my partner and I were dispatched to the scene of a jet-ski accident. Two girls were operating their jet skis at idle on the far side of the lake away from campgrounds. A wind came up and they decided to return to camp. As the first skier came on plane, the second one was coming up on plane directly behind her. The first one fell, and due to the blind spot created by the bow angle of the second ski, the operator didn't see her friend fall. She consequently pinched her between the two jet skis. Because no help

Figure 1. A Type IV ring buoy is an ideal device for a "throw" rescue. You should carry it in a convenient place, with a secure line, to be instantly available for a rescue.

was available in that remote location, the non-injured skier was forced to leave the victim and go for help. When we arrived, we observed a jet ski aground on the rocky shoreline with the victim being washed against the rocks. As we were near shore, we put the patrol boat upon the rocks and threw out our anchor on shore. We dropped gun belts, donned our PFDs, and entered the water. A quick medical assessment showed that the victim was in severe hypothermia and possibly had a broken back. We placed the victim on a backboard in the water, because an unsupported lift into our boat might have caused spinal damage. With the aid of some bystanders, we placed the victim, secured on the backboard, into our boat. While one of us operated the boat, the other treated the victim for hypothermia. A medical helicopter arrived to transport the victim to a trauma center.

This incident points up several factors that you should consider for a rescue: getting rid of the gun belt; donning PFDs; using a backboard in water before transport to the patrol craft; environmental conditions; enlisting the aid of the public; applying first-aid knowledge; having adequate first-aid equipment on board; and calling for a rescue helicopter.

In many cases, two officers cannot lift a stretcher or backboard onto a watercraft or out of the boat to a helicopter or ambulance. This is a time to enlist the aid of the public. Most of them don't mind becoming involved and will help willingly. This is another reason, however, to stow your gun belt in a secure area.

When you call for a helicopter, there are two immediate problems. If you do not have a designated helipad or are in a remote location, you must provide for a safe landing site. The other problem, in remote areas, is that of the helicopter not finding you.

The Arizona Department of Public Safety, which provides statewide helicopter medical and enforcement services, has provided a guide for the request and use of their machines. This guide stipulates a minimal landing area of 65 by 65 feet. A larger cleared area of 100 feet square is preferable. Their manual also provides the following guidelines:

> When requesting helicopter assistance give the following information to the crew:
>
> LAW ENFORCEMENT—
> 1. Type of mission.
> 2. Location and direction of travel and speed if object of search is moving.
> 3. Description of suspect, vehicle, etc.
> 4. If armed, type and number of weapons if known.
>
> MEDICAL—
> 1. Number of victims and severity of injuries.
> 2. Location: highway and milepost if applicable.
> 3. Weather at location: wind velocity and direction, rain, fog, etc.
> 4. If Hurst rescue equipment is needed, advise crew so they can load it onto helicopter.
>
> SECURITY OF HELICOPTER—
> To prevent discomfort and possible injury to bystanders, the requesting agency/officer must assist the aircrew in securing the helicopter landing zone during landing. After the helicopter is safely on the ground the pilot will assume this responsibility. However, depending upon the location and number of bystanders, he may require some assistance in providing for their safety.
>
> LANDING SITE—
> Minimum 65 by 65 feet. Desirable 100 by 100 feet. Tell the crew exactly how big the helipad is and if there are any obstructions. Also

advise them of wind speed and directions, power lines or antennae, road signs, etc., especially at night. Wires are almost impossible to see from the air. Avoid slopes of greater than eight degrees. Provide contrasting markers on snow pads. Remove all loose materials on helipad. Avoid placing command post, fires, or patient holding area near landing zones. Avoid helicopter use and landing site placement in avalanche areas. Avoid winter lakes, ponds, rivers, and sand pads.

DIRECTIONS FOR LANDING—

Raise your arms above your head, palms extended and facing forward ... then turn your back to the wind. Lower your arms horizontally and parallel to the ground, and the helicopter will land in front of you. Protect your eyes and move out of the way when the helicopter approaches.

CAUTIONS—

1. Be aware of fire hazard from road flares blown about by rotor wash.
2. Flashing lights (topmounts) can induce vertigo. Please be aware that emergency lights at the scene may cause pilot disorientation and force the helicopter to land at other than the desired landing zone. Turn them off when helicopter is landing.
3. Don't ever shine spotlights, etc., directly at helicopter. Shine them on the landing area where you want the helicopter to land.

BE ALERT AROUND THE HELICOPTER—Don't smoke in or around the helicopter without prior permission of the pilot. Don't touch the bubble or any moving parts. Ensure seat belts are inside before closing the doors. Keep well clear of landing areas when the helicopter is landing or taking off, especially with external loads. Shield your eyes near a helicopter when it is landing or taking off. Approach and leave the helicopter in a crouched manner. Never approach or leave the helicopter uphill. Always approach from the downhill side. Always avoid the blind area to the sides and rear of the helicopter, where the pilot can't see you. Always avoid the main and tail rotor system, jet exhaust and jet intake. Carry all equipment horizontally below waist level. Do not load or unload cargo from the helicopter unless directed by the flight crew. Never walk near the rear of the helicopter. Keep the landing area clean. The helicopter downwash will lift and move an amazing variety of things. Don't slam the helicopter doors but close them gently and don't let them swing in the wind. Never throw any object in the vicinity of the helicopter. Carry tools and other long objects horizontally below waist level, not upright or over the shoulder. Hold on to your hat. Don't have campfires near the landing site.

You should contact your local air rescue services and determine their needs and preferences before you request them.

As discussed above, when you request air services, they need to find your location, especially if you're in a remote area. This makes it important to carry a signaling device with you. A signal mirror works very well on sunny days. The brilliant flash will quickly disclose your exact location. Aerial flares work best on cloudy days, and smoke grenades reveal your presence as well as indicate wind direction.

The use of aeronautical charts, as provided by state transportation boards, will greatly facilitate a pilot's finding your location. These charts cover a large area and have plots of VHF omnidirectional radio range with magnetic bearings from their stations. By identifying two VHF radio facilities and triangulated compass direction from each, you can plot your position precisely. You need to think about position signal locators and make arrangements to carry them aboard your patrol watercraft.

You'll need appropriate first-aid and response equipment for rescues. We'll discuss, in the equipment section, what we feel are minimal first-aid supplies to be carried aboard a patrol watercraft.

After meeting the immediate needs, prepare your follow-up action. At this time, check with witnesses and victims in order to account for all the people involved and to determine if anyone is missing.

After you've taken care of the victims and have controlled the scene, begin your investigation as soon as possible. First, identify all witnesses. Determine what the operator(s) were doing before and during the accident. You'll need answers to at least the following questions:

1. What happened?

This is often not obvious from the accident scene. Remember that water accidents don't leave skid marks, broken headlight glass, or other physical evidence to locate the point of impact. Indeed, boats often drift away from the scene of the original mishap.

2. When did it happen?

This, too, may be hard to pin down, unless you came upon the scene within a few minutes after it happened.

3. Where did it happen?

Take wind and current into account when trying to answer this question.

4. What were the weather and water conditions?

Unless there's been a sudden change or a great lapse of time before you arrive, this answer should be self-evident.

5. Were there any other boats in the area?

It's important to know if there were additional people in the area, either involved in the accident or as witnesses.

6. Where are they now?

You need to locate them and to find out what roles they played, as witnesses or victims.

7. Were there any other witnesses who left the scene before your arrival?

Witnesses are more important than with a road accident investigation because of less physical evidence. This is why you need to locate anyone who saw the accident.

8. Were there any other victims transported to an emergency facility before your arrival?

You'll need answers to these and many other questions in order to conduct a good accident investigation and prepare an adequate report. You'll also need to collect physical evidence. After you have a good idea of how the accident took place, you'll need to draw a diagram of the accident scene. A quick sketch while on the water will be adequate, but after you get to shore and have time to produce a polished version of your report, you'll need to draw a neat diagram. A set of boating accident templates, such as the "Bear-Aide," will help you draw sharp outlines.

Because this book's focus is on officer survival tactics, we won't get deeply into watercraft accident investigation. This information is available elsewhere, and there are several good accident investigation and reconstruction training courses available.

From the viewpoint of officer survival, do not rush in to help until you thoroughly understand the situation and its dangers. Above all, do not endanger yourself or your watercraft, because if you do, you'll become part of the problem. You'll be unable to help the victims if you're injured yourself, or if your watercraft becomes disabled or sunk. At times, you'll feel that certain risks are justified, but take only those risks which yield a positive return; in other words, calculated risks. Law officers are rarely accused of cowardice. On the contrary, they have a tendency to take needless risks, even when safer courses of action are possible. Always remember that life, including your life, takes priority over property.

NOTES

1. *Two Little Words,* Steve King, EMERGENCY, January, 1990, p. 62.

Chapter 15

NIGHT OPERATIONS

Operating a patrol watercraft during poor light conditions is a severe test of seamanship. Night patrol is totally different from daytime patrol, even in the same patrol area. The feeling of unfamiliarity can be startling, almost as if you were operating in a different area.

Figure 1. During night operations the absence of light plays tricks with your eyes. Objects appear to have only two dimensions, with no color or shadows. This makes everything appear flat, altering your depth perception. Always familiarize yourself with an area during daylight before patrolling it at night.

In some instances lights will replace day markers. Therefore, you must be completely familiar with the navigational system at night as well as day. Depth perception is altered and familiar shoreline reference points become invisible. This greatly increases the potential for a mishap. Due to the dangers of lone officer survival, all night operations must have at least two officers.

Figure 2. Highly visible daytime markers become almost invisible at night, which is why you must be familiar with hazards in your patrol area. In many instances, lights replace visual markers.

Adding to the hazards of night operations is the fact that it may be impossible to establish good night vision. The watercraft marking system for vessels under 26 feet in length requires a 32-point white light aft, which must be visible for two miles. The result is a halo of white light around your patrol watercraft. If not properly shrouded, this light illuminates your cockpit, bounces off your helm and railings and may even reflect back from your windshield. If you happen to look directly at it, you will ruin your vision. It will also silhouette you and your partner.

To see adequately at night and provide officer protection, you must take some steps to mitigate this glare. Some agencies have the light mounted above a shield or boat house. Most patrol watercraft, however, are modifications of pleasure boats and have the traditional stern-mounted light. Some officers place a shield around the fore part of the light to shade the helm, but this is contrary to regulations and, in the event of an accident, makes them liable. Another choice is a two-light arrangement in which a stern light covers the rear portion of the boat and a forward-mounted light covers the front portion of the watercraft, with the helm remaining in shadow. Unfortunately, this system may hinder forward vision.

If you use a spotlight or hand-held light, you'll get glare from your boat and its bright hardware, which will ruin night vision. Radios and instruments with panel lights also contribute to the problem. In some patrol areas, surface glare from on-shore facilities and cities degrades night vision.

These sources of light pollution severely hamper your ability to adequately establish night vision. Consequently, you need to remember that your night vision will be poor and that you'll need to operate your watercraft with caution. If possible, use non-glare paint or tape to eliminate reflections. Move or shield lights as practical. During a night stop you need to be careful not to be backlit. The installation of red instruments, radio and cockpit lights will also help preserve night vision.

Keep a constant lookout for other boats and water skiers, swimmers, and water obstacles. Not all boats display lights, and often the only thing you will see will be the white foam of their wakes. Partners must quickly advise each other of potential hazards.

Some watercraft are equipped with tinted windshields. While this may be helpful on sunny days, it's a liability at night. With night vision already poor, it's like operating your watercraft wearing sunglasses.

If you have a patrol watercraft without an adequate windshield, you absolutely must find other ways to protect your eyes. A beetle ramming into your eye at 30 miles an hour may cause you to lose an eye and your career as a watercraft officer. You should carry a good grade of clear goggles and wear them during night operations, if your boat doesn't have a windshield to provide good eye and face protection. Ordinary clear glasses have the disadvantage that debris can enter from the sides. Even grains of sand from the forward deck can cause tremendous pain if they strike your eye when traveling at speed.

Many officers overlook binoculars for night use. Binoculars gather light and will provide a magnified view of a subject. You should use binoculars at night as often as during the day. You must remember, however, that the human eye sees color better in the center of field and sees black and white better around the edges. Therefore, when viewing

Figure 3. Some officers mount their boarding lights near the bow. Wherever you put yours, make sure that your lights don't silhouette you to the subjects. This patrol boat provides good light cover for its officers.

at night, don't look directly at an object but look around it, catching it in your peripheral vision. When you see it, don't stare at it, but use a circular eye motion. This provides better visual acuity and is a good technique with or without binoculars.

Night vision devices have been coming down in price, making them more affordable for most government agencies. There are two basic reasons for use of these devices. One is for operation of watercraft, with the operator wearing night vision goggles. The other reason is surveillance.

Piloting vessels with goggles requires no magnification. However, the field of vision is restricted. For surveillance, a magnifying hand-held monocular or binocular type works well, especially if it has a camera adapter. Both systems work best with no external artificial light. Their sensitivity requires that they shut down when they are pointed towards bright light, and an internal circuit does this automatically in second-generation and later models. Because of light pollution from other boats and campgrounds, we have found these devices to have limited application. When they work well, they're very useful, but they are not suitable for all night activities.

Many agencies use hand-held lights as lighting for operations or when boarding another vessel. These provide quite a bit of light, especially if they're equal in brightness to an aircraft landing light. Their drawback for boarding operations is that they're hand-held, which causes the cover officer to lose the use of one hand. This can be awkward, because it prevents him from effectively using a long gun as backup cover during high-risk boardings.

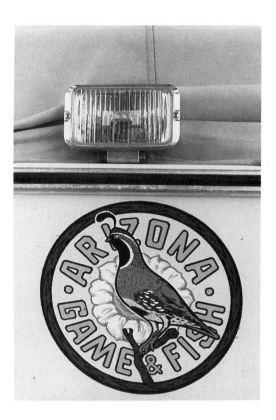

Figure 4. Gunnel-mounted boarding lights free your hands for more important work. A major problem with any light is that it can serve as an aiming point if a suspect opens fire. You must mount them away from the helm to avoid drawing gunfire directly to your location. This patrol boat has both the agency logo and boarding light mounted about two feet in front of the operator's position.

A better solution is to equip your patrol watercraft with light mounts or permanently mounted boarding lights. Two quartz-halogen flood lights mounted on the port and starboard gunnels (operated with independent switches) provide plenty of light for nighttime boardings. Your hands will be free and you'll be able to pay more attention to the subjects instead of being preoccupied with placement of the lights.

If you mount such lights on your patrol watercraft, take care to place them away from your position. If a suspect shoots at your boat, you don't want to be sitting behind a bright aiming point! You should also keep this point in mind when holding a spotlight. Hold it out and away from you, and forget about those trendy "flashlight shooting stances" you may have seen in the gun magazines. Holding sidearm and flashlight together in front of your body merely ensures that the aiming point you give a suspect is center mass.

Some officers have obtained small goose-necked pocket lights for use during night operations. When issuing a citation, they attached the light to their shirt or PFD. The adjustable small light provides perfect illumination for the citation and frees both hands. If the light is too bright, it is usually shaded with red plastic. This prevents the reflected light from the citation from completely ruining night vision. A high-intensity flashlight is advantageous for lighting up an area, but the brightness becomes a deadly handicap if it causes you to become night blind when focusing on nearby objects.

Each officer on night operations should wear a well-fitting PFD, because a fall overboard into dark water could be fatal. Most such falls usually occur due to a mishap involving an accident or physical confrontation. Either way, you risk striking your head on a hard object, and without a PFD, your chances for survival are minimal. In cold water, a Type III float coat, or survival suit, is preferable.

The watercraft operator should also attach the kill switch lanyard to his PFD during night operations. You must have an extra kill switch in the boat and you must make sure your partner knows its location. If the operator goes overboard with the lanyard attached, you cannot operate the boat to come to his assistance without another switch.

Finding an overboard officer in the water at night is a very difficult, if not impossible, operation. This is why there should be a strobe light attached to all PFD's worn. There are several versions of personal strobes which range in price from expensive to affordable. One of the best is a watertight strobe powered by one "D" cell battery and which is not much bigger than its power source. It has a very bright strobe bulb and a large clip to secure it to a PFD. If you have one of these attached to your PFD and can turn it on, your location will be readily visible. Some of the more expensive strobes will turn on automatically if wet. These may be preferable if you can afford them.

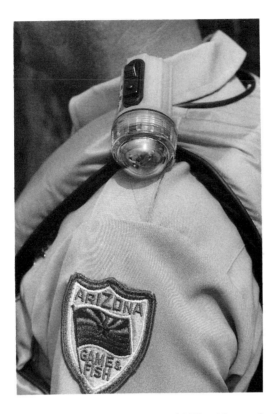

Figure 5. During night patrol, you should wear a good PFD with a strobe light attached. This one can be activated by the officer, so that his location will be known should he go overboard.

If it becomes necessary to board at night, you should always display a blue light and make sure you identify yourself to the occupants of the other boat. Approaches by patrol boats are not normal boating activity and the darkness prevents the subjects from seeing who you are. Their concern for personal safety is certainly understandable. You must reveal your identity, authority and intentions to them as soon as possible. Your uniform should be visible, and PFD's should be marked with your agency insignia. It's wise to use some type of boarding lights, in order to light up the subject's boat and dazzle the occupants, making any hostile actions more difficult. Experience shows that there is a high probability of firearms being aboard boats at night. Also, poachers have been known to jacklight game from boats or to run illegal netting operations.

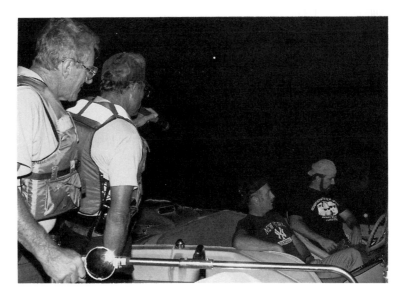

Figure 6. Public contacts during night operations are common. Darkness aids the subjects, and officers must use their lights in order to gain and retain a tactical advantage.

The blue light, especially if it's a multidirectional strobe, is blinding. To avoid being dazzled, you should use a shield, such as a canvas bag with a clear plastic insert sewn in to cover the strobe. This shields you from the light but makes it visible to the other boat.

If you do a lot of night work, it may be helpful to obtain some aerial parachute flares, available from police equipment suppliers. The flare comes in a stout cardboard tube. Upon firing, it propels a bright flare hundreds of feet into the air and floats down slowly under a parachute. This device provides a lot of instant light. Usually, subjects will look at it, losing their night vision, thus giving you an additional advantage. These replace the old military 35mm flare guns and have many uses, including search and rescue work, pursuits, and nighttime felony boardings.

Also handy to have on board are some small hand-held fishermen marker buoys. These can be immediately deployed if the suspects dump evidence during a pursuit. You can find them later without much difficulty and they will help you find the ditched evidence.[1]

Pursuits should be from far port or starboard. Due to the high risks of night stops, any craft who flees from you should be treated as a high-speed felony stop which was described earlier in this chapter.

Figure 7. A canvas light cover prevents this strobe light from dazzling officers during a night operation.

NOTES

1. *International Game Warden,* Summer, 1987, Michael Duran "Wildlife Officer Survival, Part II."

Chapter 16

BOOBY TRAPS

Officers who may encounter illegal drug smugglers or marijuana growers have to beware of alarms and booby traps. Stepped-up enforcement in cities has caused growers to move into remote areas, where enforcement is sparse. Many of these lie in federal or state recreation areas. Marijuana growers protect their "gardens" with booby traps and/or alarms for several purposes:

1. To warn of anyone approaching.
2. To obstruct access.
3. To impede or delay police pursuit.[1]

Some booby traps are aimed directly at game and fish officers. Ragnar Benson describes in his book, *Survival Poaching,* how he and his uncle rigged a booby trap against state game wardens. They used rope to suspend four sticks about 12 feet above the water, using a battery and electrical cap to ignite the dynamite. A mousetrap with a length of wire crossing the river and attached to the crossbar served as the trigger. Fortunately, the explosion did not kill anyone.[2]

There are many types of alarms and booby traps. These are dangerous, and unless you've taken an explosive ordinance disposal course, don't try to tamper with any you find. Your survival will depend on learning to recognize them and avoiding them when you do.

In an unfamiliar area, move very slowly and watch for wires, strings, and filament line. Any fine wire or string, running anywhere between throat and ankle level, can trigger an alarm or booby trap. If you see one of these, freeze! Just stop in your tracks and look around carefully to see where it leads. Never forget that you may have already stepped over one end of a convoluted wire layout, and that backing off along the same path may bring you into it again. The wire may lead to a firearm pointed down the path or to an explosive charge. It may also pull down an incendiary bomb.[3]

An alarm/booby trap can be very simple. A few fish hooks, strung on monofilament fishing line at face level, will cause a world of hurt. Anyone running into this will scream and thrash around, making enough noise to alert the person who set the trap.

Some booby traps are in the ground itself. A hole dug into the trail, with the opening camouflaged, will break your leg if you fall into it. There may be sharp stakes at the bottom to increase the injury.

To avoid this type of trap, look for freshly dug earth and for bumps and irregularities in the forest floor. Look for a carpet of fallen leaves where none would ordinarily be. Look for anything artificial, such as pieces of metal or plastic pipe. Probe the trail ahead of you with a stick or with your baton. If you're a member of a raiding party against a known site, also probe the sides of the trail. Some booby trappers will put traps there to catch anyone seeking cover in a hurry. They may also booby-trap an object of compelling interest, such as a firearm laying on the ground. Never pick one up, until you're sure its safe.

Most importantly, if you suspect booby traps may be present, don't go in alone. You may need a backup officer to rescue you if you're injured. Also, approach in daylight. It's too easy to run into a booby trap in darkness, and you don't want to advertise your position by using a flashlight. Wear your body armor, as well. It can stop some projectiles.

If you find anything which suggests a booby trap, do not, repeat, do not try to disarm it. Send for an EOD technician. Remember that, even if you succeed in disarming the device, a suspect may attack you while your attention is totally engaged in that delicate task.

You may have to be ruthless. If you capture suspects whom you think may have laid booby traps, have them walk in front of you so that they'll trip any trap they set. In such a situation, watch their footsteps carefully, because they may step over a trip wire, leaving it for you.

NOTES

1. Lyman, Michael D., *Narcotics and Crime Control.* Springfield, Illinois, Charles C Thomas, 1987, p. 124.
2. Benson, Ragnar, *Survival Poaching.* Boulder, Colorado, Paladin, 1980, pp. 16–17.
3. Mullins, Wayman C., *Terrorist Organizations in the United States.* Springfield, Illinois, Charles C Thomas, 1988, pp. 134–135.

Chapter 17

ENVIRONMENTAL SURVIVAL

Patrol Environment Hazards

U nlike a land patrol officer's beat, the watercraft patrol officer's work area is always on a hostile environment. Only the patrol boat keeps the officer from facing a grim situation in the water. Usually, in discussing "officer survival," we think about traditional dangers posed by the criminal, but officer survival really means going home safely after your shift. To accomplish this, we must consider the total working environment, and for a watercraft patrol officer, a deadly environment is the water on which he works. Proof of this lies in the many examples of officers drowning while on watercraft patrol.

In his video, "The Reasons People Drown," Doctor Frank Pia points out that drowning is the second cause of accidental death for people between the ages of 1 to 44. He also describes the "instinctive drowning response" which is exhibited by drowning victims. According to Doctor Pia, a person in distress in the water can call out for help and can swim or float. Contrary to present misconceptions of drowning, an actual drowning victim cannot get enough air to call out for help because the victim is suffocating and does not have enough air to make any noise. Instead, involuntary movements take over and the victim's extended arms move up and down, splashing the water around him in an attempt to keep his head out of the water. He cannot wave for help and his head is held high. For an adult, the struggle lasts for only 20 to 60 seconds, until the victim drowns. Observers often think the person is playing and fail to recognize the danger. This is what makes it critical for you to observe and correctly evaluate what you see when you encounter a drowning. This information can also help you avoid the conditions that lead to drowning, so that if you fall into the water you'll have a better chance of surviving.

If you are in a position to aid the victim, remember the various techniques of "Reach, Throw, Row, and Go" discussed earlier. Also realize that a person with the instinctive drowning response cannot aid

Figure 1. During watercraft operations, you usually do not have the luxury of exiting your patrol vehicle in order to gain a tactical advantage. The patrol environment itself provides a hazardous situation.

himself. Any rescue device must be placed under his thrashing arms quickly. Doctor Pia also states that most drownings occur within 10 to 15 feet of safety. Alcohol, cold water, and cold air all increase the chances of drowning.

Learning how people drown is helpful, and watching Doctor Pia's videotape provides vivid insights into the dynamics of this process. This is a very powerful video presentation and we feel that it should be required viewing for all watercraft patrol officers.

Another problem is falling overboard and you should do all you can to avoid this. Knowledge of the causes of drowning, effects of hypothermia, basic lifesaving techniques, and the use of safety equipment will assist you if you do happen to fall in.

In cold wind and water conditions, you should wear a Type III float coat or survival suit. You should also be prepared to drop your gun belt, without hesitation and without thought of what it'll cost you to replace it. When you're in the water, gun belt "keepers" may prevent you from shedding this weight. This is why we recommend not using keepers while on watercraft patrol.

During night operations, you should always wear a PFD with a strobe light attached. If working in hazardous conditions (waves, wind, night, and pursuits), you should wear a Type I PFD. These are the only PFDs that will reliably turn your face up and out of the water if you're unconscious.

Your boat should be equipped with a boarding ladder or swim platforms. Without them, you might find it very difficult to board your boat after a fall overboard, especially if alone.

Putting on a PFD in deep water is an extremely difficult task. You should be a good swimmer and comfortable in the water. Take advantage of local swimming and rescue courses. Practice swimming in your uniform in order to get the feel of it wet, as this will help prevent panic later. Also practice putting on different types of PFDs in deep water. When you do this, practice in a controlled environment with a partner who can aid you if you need help.

If you cannot swim or are afraid of the water, take lessons and learn. If you don't want to do this, get a transfer. Although it may seem silly, there are watercraft officers who can't swim.

Learn the basic rescue techniques of Reach, Throw, Row and Go. Obtain and wear a good-fitting Type I PFD and be observant of dangerous situations.

Hypothermia (i.e. loss of body heat) is a serious danger for the watercraft patrol officer, because it can occur in any climate. You must keep yourself as warm and as dry as possible at all times. Water will leach heat from your body 25 times faster than air, and 50 percent of body heat can be lost from your head alone, according to Doctor Pia. According to the Department of the Air Force Survival Training Manual, "The greatest problem a survivor is faced with when submerged in cold water is death due to hypothermia. When a survivor is immersed in cold water, hypothermia occurs rapidly due to the decreased insulating quality of wet clothing and the fact that water displaces the layer of still air which normally surrounds the body. Water causes a rate of heat exchange approximately 25 times greater than air at the same temperature."

Your survival expectancy varies with water temperature. For instance, if the water temperature is between 60 to 70 degrees Fahrenheit, your survival expectancy is 12 hours. Between 50 to 60 degrees, it drops to six hours. Between 40 to 50 degrees, you have one hour and if the temperature is 40 degrees or lower, less than one hour. A survival suit will increase these times.

You should not remove wet clothing when immersed in water, because they still provide some insulation. Once out of the water, discard wet clothes and put on dry clothing. If you can't, the fallback plan is to remove them, wring them out and put them back on.

You don't have to be immersed in water to suffer from hypothermia. If you get wet, the evaporative effect of the wind on your clothes will cause you to lose body heat rapidly because of the "chill factor." Heavy exercise in cold climates may cause body sweat to wet clothing and increase heat loss. Placing your body against a cold object without insulation can also cause a drop in your temperature. Wind can also be a significant cause of heat loss, even if you're dry, again because of the chill factor.

The best safeguard against hypothermia is to understand how it comes about and how to prevent it. Symptoms of hypothermia include:

SHIVERING, which is uncontrollable. This is an attempt by your body to increase its heat.

LOSS OF AWARENESS occurs next and this includes confusion of thought, speech difficulties, and amnesia.

STIFFNESS of muscles occurs after shivering and, in this stage, the victim looks bluish, puffy and semi-conscious.

The PULSE SLOWS and in the extremities it is almost undetectable.

UNCONSCIOUSNESS occurs, with dilation of the pupils and an erratic heartbeat. This state comes about when the body core temperature drops to around 86 degrees Fahrenheit.

RELAXATION of muscles throughout the body is the next phase.

CARDIAC FAILURE is the final stage, as the body core temperature drops too low to sustain life.[1]

As a watercraft officer, you need to detect these symptoms in both a rescued victim and yourself. As this is not a first-aid book, we suggest that your first-aid training include a good coverage of hypothermia.

The best way of dealing with hypothermia is prevention. Keep yourself from getting wet or cold. Even in the summer desert, watercraft patrol officers have suffered from hypothermia while operating during moderate and high winds, which caused spray to wet the officers and then chilled their wet clothing.

You should have a good set of issue rain gear. Regardless of your patrol area, all officers should also be issued a flotation coat and/or a survival suit. These are also called anti-exposure suits. These coats and suits are heavily insulated and provide a high degree of protection from wind and water.

Use head coverings, as a great deal of heat is lost from the head. Also protect your hands, feet, nose, and ears. Try to conserve body heat and augment it by drinking hot liquids if you can. Exercise, move around, stretch and keep your blood circulating rapidly.

Loose-fitting clothing is preferable to tight clothing, as it gives more air space for insulation, but it should not be so loose as to allow wind drafts. Finally, control your sweating if you are working in cold climates.

If you begin to shiver uncontrollably, remove yourself immediately from the source of your heat loss. Do not delay, because mental confusion follows quickly and your delay may cause you to become mentally incapable of saving yourself. Also remember that wind chill will create additional heat losses, and the wind, even if it feels warm, coupled with wet clothing, will chill you quickly.

Replace your wet clothing, get out of the wind, and keep dry. Warming the body from the inside is the best way to treat hypothermia. If possible, induce warmth into the core of the body through warm liquids or breathing warm air.

If you are still cold and warm liquids are not available, body-to-body contact may be necessary. Exercise will also help raise your temperature. Above all, DO NOT consume any alcohol. This may make you feel warm but causes your blood vessels to dilate, especially at the surface, allowing your core blood to be cooled in your extremities. Using tobacco, whether by smoking or chewing, also impedes recovery, because nicotine causes your blood vessels to constrict and interferes with circulation.

Avoid paradoxical cooling. This happens when you warm your body from the outside, but your inner core temperature is still dropping. Warmth from the inside, such as warm liquids, is best.

Another environmental condition that affects watercraft patrol officers is dehydration. While surrounded by water, you may not feel the need to drink fluids. You also may not be aware that wind causes perspiration to evaporate quickly, and you may not notice the amount of fluid loss through sweating. You may fail to compensate for this fluid loss and suffer dehydration. One way of monitoring your fluid state is to watch for symptoms, which include headache, acute thirst, dry mouth, loss of appetite, apathy, drowsiness, cracked lips, slow speech, and weakness.

Prevention is as simple as drinking water and wearing protective clothing. You should make sure to drink fluids whether you feel thirsty or not. If you realize that you are dehydrated, drink some fluid immediately, but avoid alcohol, nicotine and salty drinks. If in a hot climate, get into the shade and avoid any strenuous activity.

Three other environmental problems that may affect you include the effects of excessive heat: sunstroke, heat exhaustion, and heat cramps. All are preventable by keeping up your fluid intake and monitoring your salt loss. If you work in hot climates, such as the Southwest desert waters, you and your watercraft should be equipped with with a shade, such as a Bimini top or a "T" top. You should wear loose clothing and carry cold drinks. You should also be completely familiar with the initial symptoms of these conditions and be prepared to take immediate action when you recognize them.

One time I was working out of Willow Beach on the Colorado River during a July patrol and our craft was not provided with a shade. The air temperature was over 110 degrees. After a couple of hours my partner and I both began to feel nauseous, which made us realize that we were overheated. We beached the boat, removed our gun belts and waded into the water. When we felt cool again, we returned to the dock and ended our shift.

Occasionally, you'll find that wind and weather conditions are so bad that it's better to stay in the marina. Unless you have a compelling reason to venture out, it's prudent to remain in shelter. Watercraft officers on Lake Mead are advised to carry MREs (Meal, Ready to Eat) and a sleeping bag on their patrol boats. Summer storms are so severe, and can occur so quickly, that the best survival technique is to go to a lee shore and wait out the storm.

"In Water" Survival

If you go into the water, there are several steps you must take to save your life. As a precaution, make sure there is a backup kill switch in your boat and that your partner knows where to find it. As mentioned earlier, if you go overboard with the kill switch attached, your partner won't be able to start the boat to come to your rescue.

If you're ejected from a boat you're operating while it's under power, the craft may turn and run you down if you don't have a kill switch attached. If your partner is alert, he'll bring the boat under control.

There have been several instances in which an out-of-control boat has turned and run over the operator in the water.

If working at night, be sure you have a strobe light attached to your PFD and wear a Type I PFD. Activate it once in the water in order to allow rescuers to find you. A Type I will float you face-up in case you become disoriented or are knocked out when you go overboard.

Once you're in the water and there is no danger from your boat, the following actions are recommended:

1. If close to shore or a boat, get out of the water as soon as possible to protect yourself from hypothermia.
2. You may have to shed heavy or bulky items, such as your gun belt. Retain your clothing, as it will help keep you warm in the water.
3. Avoid unnecessary swimming. It consumes energy and increases your heat loss.
4. Float on the surface in a HELP (heat escape lessening posture) position to conserve body heat.
5. If more than one person, group together to help conserve body heat.
6. Keep your morale up and retain the will to survive.
7. Keep as much of your body out of the water as possible and avoid panic.[2]
8. Wearing a flotation device will help conserve body heat and save energy.
9. As your head will lose up to 50 percent of your body heat, keep your head as far out of the water as possible. Keep your back turned to the wind and waves.[3]
10. Assuming the HELP position will increase your survival time. The HELP position is achieved by crossing your legs and drawing them up into a fetal position and remaining still. High areas of heat loss are the head, neck, sides and groin.
11. If in the water without a life preserver, remember that air trapped in clothing will help buoy you in the water. If in the water for a long time, you will have to rest from treading water. This is best accomplished by floating on your back. If you wish to travel, use the following technique: "Rest erect in the water and inhale; put the head face-down in the water and stroke with the arms; rest in this face-down position until there is a need to breath again; raise

the head and exhale; support the body by kicking arms and legs and inhaling; then repeat the cycle."[4]

12. Swimming with a life preserver: Wearing a PFD adds bulk to your body and creates drag in the water. It also provides flotation to keep your head out of the water and lets you conserve energy you would be using keeping afloat. Conserving energy and keeping your head out of the water decrease your heat loss and thus increase your survival time. The best way to swim, while wearing a PFD, is on your back using the backstroke. When you approach the shore or a boat, turn over and use the breaststroke. If you are wearing a float coat, make sure you deploy the groin protector properly and promptly. The built-in hood should be secured over your head. Both of these actions will significantly reduce heat loss. If you are wearing an exposure suit, make sure to wear it correctly, hood deployed, zippers and flaps fastened. With both float coats and survival suits, float and swim on your back, as with a regular PFD. Some survival suits come with a self-inflating collar, which you should inflate to help keep your head out of the water.

NOTES

1. Farley, M., and Huff, R., *Sea Survival: The Boatman's Emergency Manual.* PA, Tab Books Inc., 1989, pp. 67–68.
2. House, D.J., *Marine Survival and Rescue Systems.* Maryland, Cornell Maritime Press, 1988, Section 1.6.
3. Farley, p. 64.
4. *Survival Training,* U.S. Air Force Volume I, 15 July, 1985, p. 451.

Chapter 18

TOWING WATERCRAFT

There will be several situations in which you will find it necessary to tow watercraft. Seized or disabled boats, or boats with the operator under arrest and with no one else to operate it, will probably comprise most of your towing needs. On a couple of occasions, for instance, officers have found it necessary to tow boats away from burning campgrounds.

If a suspect is under the influence of narcotics or alcohol and his passengers are incapable of operation, you cannot allow him to operate his boat any further. Your actions will take sound judgment, as you take on responsibility for his passengers. Their safety and welfare must be uppermost in your mind, especially if there are children involved.

Towing astern is the easiest technique to use, but it takes some preparation and knowledge of its limitations. You must have a tow harness, consisting of two pieces of heavy-duty line. The first piece, called the bridle, attaches across the width of your transom and fastens with snap hooks to each of your transom towing eyes. The bridle should be long enough to extend past your engine and prop. Ideally, it's three to five times the width of your transom.

The main part of the harness consists of a single heavy-duty line 15 to 25 feet in length or long enough so that if you stop, the towed vessel doesn't overtake and ram your boat. One end has a snap hook for securing on the bow eye of the boat to be towed. Its other end is secured in a non-closing loop through which the bridle passes. Immediately behind this loop is a float, which keeps the harness away from the propeller in case there's any slack in the line.

To deploy, you first attach the bridle to the patrol watercraft's transom. You then attach the towline to the subject's boat. As your patrol craft slowly pulls away, one officer feeds out the towline by hand, being careful not to get it wrapped around a hand or leg. You slowly pull away until you can drop the float out and away from your prop. You then take up slack and begin towing. Build up speed gradually to avoid snapping the line. The speed of the towing operation should be such that you

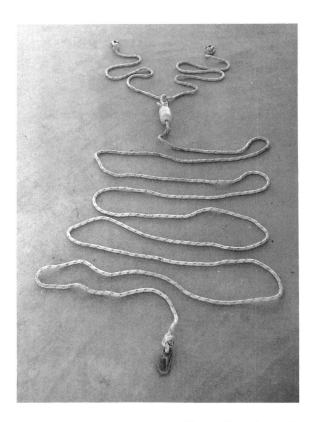

Figure 1. Every patrol boat should be equipped with a well-made tow harness. Its length depends on local conditions. A float keeps the bridle away from the propeller.

establish control over the towed boat, so that the towed boat will not overrun your craft because of wind or waves.

When making course corrections, use gradual turns. The loop will slide along the bridle, giving you better pull over the tow, and gradual turns will place less stress on the line and give you greater control.

You should keep even tension on the towline at all times. Do not allow slack to come into the line, as you do not want to foul your prop in the harness. The float is there to help keep the bridle and loop at the surface of the water. If slack occurs, do not "snatch" the line, but gradually bring it taut.

If you must tow, ensure that all persons involved, prisoners, passengers, suspects, subjects and officers, are wearing PFDs.

When towing, use your blue or emergency lights, and if possible tow to the closest harbor. In bad weather, avoid towing with the wind or waves at your stern or broadside to them. If your patrol boat is large enough, it's best to have all passengers board your boat and secure safe seating before beginning your tow. Towing with passengers remaining in the towed boat can be hazardous, unless it's large enough to afford them protection. Remember that life is more important than property.

If towing at night, turn on the tow's lights or illuminate it with your spotlight.

Towing of jet skis is difficult. They have a tendency to roll and be damaged. If you must tow one, use caution and slow speeds.

When you complete your tow, take up the bridle. Don't unfasten it, but pull it in until you have the line clear of the prop. Pull in the bridle and then pull in the towline until you can unhook the snap from the subject's bow eye.

There are some disadvantages to towing astern and you should be familiar with them.

1. Control of the towed boat is difficult when in a harbor or beach, as you have no way to steer the other boat. It will turn inside your turns, so delicate maneuvers are difficult.

2. You must constantly keep an eye on the tow as well as maintaining a good forward lookout.

3. Towing in rough water is dangerous, as you don't have positive control over the towed boat. A wave or wind can slam it into your hull.

4. If you have a prisoner, your attention will be divided as you approach shore. As he gets closer to jail and to shore, he may attempt to escape. Your tow will require your full attention. Make sure you and your partner are aware of this. The operator should worry about the tow and the partner worry about the suspect.

Chapter 19

ASSAULTS ON THE WATER

Assault Information

There are no national information sources covering assaults on water-craft officers. The best reference available is the yearly publication prepared by the U.S. Department of the Interior's Fish and Wildlife Service, Division of Law Enforcement. This is titled *Conservation Officers Killed and Assaulted.* They have been producing this report for two years, and both 1988 and 1989 editions are now in circulation. As its title suggests, the information is oriented towards conservation officers. Across the United States, many other officers perform watercraft patrol duties, and therefore the listing does not include all watercraft officer assaults. However, the publication provides valuable insights on the types of assaults a watercraft officer can expect to face.

In both 1987 and 1988, personal weapons (fists, feet, etc.) were the most frequently used weapons for assaults. Of the 103 assaults reported in 1988, 50% of the assaults involved personal weapons. Firearms comprised 22%, and 15% were with vehicles. The remainder, 13%, involved unspecified weapons, and one knife attack was reported. In 1987, 128 assaults fell into these categories; personal weapons, 34%; firearms, 32%; and vehicles, 18%. Of the remainder, seven suspects used knives, five used other types of weapons, and in nine assaults the weapon was not identified.

The figures also break down the types of activities leading to these assaults. Hunting license checks received the highest assault rate (17%). Fishing license checks (14%) and routine patrol (13%) were the second and third most common activities leading to assaults in 1988. Of the 103 assaults reported, five were during routine boating safety checks. Nine were during routine fishing checks and 13 during routine patrol. The data for 1987 showed two assaults during boating safety checks (1.6%) and 17 attacks during routine fishing checks (13.3%).

In 1988, 44% of the assaults were against officers working alone and

35% involved pairs or teams of officers. In 1987, the team assignment had a higher assault rate (45%), while single-officer incidents were 42%. There were two officers killed in 1987, one during a routine fisherman check, but none in 1988.

In the Summer, 1985 issue of the *International Game Warden* magazine, an article titled "In Memory" contains these incidents of water-based enforcement officers killed on duty: "...beaten to death by fisherman....," "...found shot to death in his boat...," "...killed in same incident, found shot to death in his boat...," "...was boarding boat of a suspected violator when he was shot...," "...shot by 17-year-old suspect who was fishing without a license...," "...drowned under mysterious circumstances and believed to have been killed...," "...killed by a man whom he was arresting for littering a stream without realization that subject was wanted...."

Recently, in Arizona there were two watercraft officers assaulted. One involved an Arizona Game and Fish Officer who was assaulted with personal weapons while issuing citations for an inoperable fire extinguisher and insufficient PFDs. This occurred at Lee's Ferry on the Colorado River. The suspect was arrested and there was no injury to the officer.

The other incident had a more serious ending. Two National Park Rangers, on watercraft patrol at the Lake Mead National Recreational Area, were attacked by a knife-wielding suspect. After attempts to disarm the assailant, the suspect boarded the patrol boat and attacked them. The officers escaped injury only by shooting him. Later, the suspect was determined to be a manic-depressive who had stopped taking his medicine while out camping.

Although the assault rate against conservation officers is generally lower than attacks on other police officers, some trends have become obvious over the years. The rate of assaults with personal weapons and firearms is close to that against city police, but firearms assaults on conservation officers usually involve more powerful weapons. Also, it appears that the ambush rate against conservation officers is slightly higher than that against other officers.

Despite there being no nationwide information available on assaults against watercraft officers, it's fair to assume that we will be assaulted with personal weapons, firearms and edged weapons. Obviously, our training and tactics should deal with these threats.

Defensive Tactics

Use of personal weapons leads the list of assaults. Your ability to use effective countermeasures will help you survive this type of attack. Knowledge and practice of suitable techniques will provide you with confidence and skill.

Many agencies have use-of-force policies. These typically address the escalation-of-force principle and authorize using sufficient force to accomplish the arrest. Normally, policies allow using one level of force higher than the suspect employs, providing that it's appropriate to the situation.

Many escalation-of-force charts start with verbal control techniques. If these fail and the suspect begins physical resistance, you can use empty-hand techniques against him. If he uses personal weapons against you, your appropriate response is to use intermediate impact tools or chemical control agents. Some of these devices are the collapsible baton, straight baton, Kubotan, flashlight, and the side-handle baton. The next level is deadly force. In most states, the use of deadly force is restricted to protecting your life or the life of someone else. Others also allow use of deadly force to stop a felony in progress.

In dangerous situations, you must remember that "intermediate" impact weapons can also serve to exert deadly force. If the attacker is so close that there's not time to draw the sidearm, a blow to the head or neck may be the only possible countermove that you can use in time to stop the attack. To survive encounters with violent suspects, you must become proficient in open-hand and intermediate defensive tactics and practice their use in the confines of your patrol boat.

Edged Weapons

Knives and other edged weapons are a certain component of any pleasure boat outing. Fish fillet knives are always present in tackle boxes, which is why watercraft officers can expect to encounter them, just as land-based game officers regularly meet armed hunters.

There is an extremely interesting and informative video produced by Calibre Press, "Surviving Edged Weapons," which deals with defense against blade wielders. This presentation points out that a minimum safe reaction distance from a suspect armed with an edged weapon is 21 feet. Closer than this does not give an officer time to draw his sidearm, fire and stop the suspect before the suspect can close the gap and reach the officer. The video also points out the many dangers of edged weapons and condemns the cavalier attitude many have towards the knife.

Unfortunately, patrol boats don't have much room to maintain distance from an attacker armed with an edged weapon. Reactive distances of 21 feet are rare and maneuver room is limited. You must keep a close watch for edged weapons and always consider them as serious threats. A knife is a deadly weapon and you should never deal with a knife by keeping your sidearm in your holster. An important tactic in cramped quarters is using obstacles to buy time. You can use the physical layout of your boat to obstruct the adversary's access to you. If you use the console or other part of your boat to keep the suspect from getting to you quickly, you can use the time to draw your sidearm.

Patrol Firearms

There's a significant difference between shooting on dry land and on the water. Land-based police rarely fire from a moving vehicle, but on the water, both the gun platform and the target are unstable and, indeed, may be moving quickly. The water officer usually must fire from his vehicle. Land-based officers can leave theirs and take cover behind the engine or nearby objects, but the watercraft officer can't simply jump out and find cover and a stable platform.

Many agencies are rapidly converting to high-capacity semi-autos. These modern pistols are much easier to reload and have a higher cartridge capacity. Despite the trend, revolvers continue to serve well for watercraft officers. In all cases, bullet placement is more important than firepower, and the watercraft officer must have good shooting skills and confidence in his sidearm. Whichever firearm you carry, always remember that if you miss with the first six, you may not do any better with follow-up shots.

Often, your sidearm is the only firearm on the scene, which makes it important to safeguard it. You must adopt the habit of never turning your sidearm towards subjects, because this exposes it to "snatching." Most public encounters don't turn into struggles for the firearm, but if you make it a habit to keep your gun side away from subjects, you'll be one step ahead if you meet an assaultive person.

Another point relates to pulling alongside other boats. You must never become so intent on holding boats together that you expose your

Figure 1. You must be mentally and physically prepared to defend your life and the lives of others. Proper training, planning and tactical awareness are all necessary for survival. You must practice firing from your watercraft, because you have very few other choices in a gunfight.

sidearm to capture. Be especially careful to keep your sidearm turned away when handling prisoners.

A secure holster helps firearm retention. However, remember to try the holster for ease of draw before buying it. Some "security holsters" are so secure that an officer has a very hard time extracting his sidearm when he needs it. Once you decide on the holster you want, practice drawing from it until you can withdraw the firearm smoothly. You should also practice in your patrol uniform. If you normally wear a heavy coat or survival suit, practice the draw while wearing it. For safety's sake, lets remember to empty the firearm first.

Another problem is whether or not to use keepers. Land-based officers habitually use keepers to retain their gun belts, but these can be dangerous if you fall overboard and have to discard your gun belt quickly to save your life. Remove your keepers when starting a shift on the water and be mentally prepared to sacrifice your equipment belt to save your life.

Shotguns with a "riot barrel" are effective long guns for watercraft officers. Many officers find a long gun easier to use than a sidearm, partly because of the increased control provided by supporting the

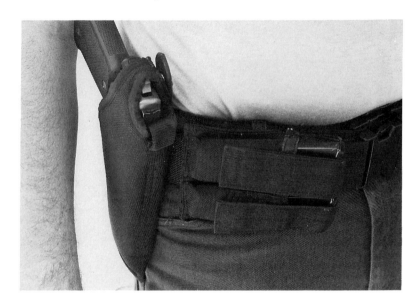

Figure 2. A nylon horizontal, or "lay-down," magazine pouch, by Eagle Industries, is helpful for two reasons. The magazines don't jab you in the ribs when you're seated or bending over, and the magazines are tilted towards the reloading hand.

firearm with both hands and the shoulder. This is the "three-point" system that offers more stability.

Shotguns offer a choice of ammunition types. Rifled slugs serve to penetrate boat hulls and deny a suspect cover. Buckshot, with multiple projectiles, improves the chances of a hit. At ranges up to about seven yards, riot shotguns shoot a very tight pattern with both birdshot and buckshot. Beyond, the pellets spread and there is a better chance of a hit. At 40 to 50 yards, the pattern has usually spread too much to be effective.

Pattern density varies with the type of ammunition, shot size and barrel characteristics. You should pattern your shotgun at various ranges with various shot, such as #1 and #4 buck, to become familiar with its performance. Over a distance, shot patterns enlarge, and you should know at what range your shotgun becomes ineffective with the shot size you're using. Also keep in mind the risk to unintended targets.

The shotgun is versatile, because it also functions well as a platform for a variety of other devices. It can be used to launch gas grenades, or penetrating "Ferret" rounds that spray liquid CN or CS inside a cabin.

The police rifle is gaining acceptance as the long gun of choice for many officers. Although its range is long and penetration deep compared to a sidearm or shotgun, officers like it for its precision, power and range. A carbine or light rifle style with high cartridge capacity and semi-auto fire is emerging as an ideal police weapon in sparsely populated areas. Favorites seem to be the Ruger Mini-14, Colt AR-15 and Car-15, all firing the .223 Remington cartridge.

Whichever firearms you select for watercraft enforcement, you must ensure that you maintain them well. A habit of regular cleaning and maintenance must be your goal. Waterborne duty is hard on equipment and you can't afford to have your firearm fail in time of need. Holsters and scabbards need as much attention as your firearm, and you should discard any worn, abused and misused items for your own safety.

The basic principle of firearms use is the same as with any other tool: "It's not what you've got, it's what you do with it that counts." Obviously, you must be proficient with all of your firearms. In addition to required training and qualification, you must make the effort to practice and improve your skills. Have you ever fired from your boat? Have you ever shot at a target bobbing on the water from your boat? Have you used cover while shooting from your boat? Can you reliably strike the center of mass on a target between seven and 15 yards with a sidearm? Have you tested your skill at hitting targets out to 100 yards? Can you access your long gun and deploy it quickly? Have you patterned your shotgun at various ranges with your duty loads? Is your slug barrel sighted in? Have you ever practiced reloading your firearm while behind cover on your boat? Have you practiced team shooting and boat-handling techniques with your partner? Can you draw and fire two rounds in less than two seconds, preferably in a second and a half? Have you ever fired your firearms under stressful conditions? Is your holster grab-resistant? Can you employ effective countermeasures to keep your sidearm secured in your holster? Do you have an established routine for firearm cleaning and maintenance inspections? Do you have an established routine for holster and leather maintenance? If you can't answer yes to these questions, you should seriously reevaluate your personal training and performance.

Cover and Concealment

We all remember the difference between cover and concealment. Cover shields you from both view and gunfire, while concealment only hides you. Both are critical in a gunfight.

In every training class and every tactical survival book, you will learn to seek cover or concealment, return fire, and exit the kill zone. Let's discuss cover first. In order to test just how much cover our watercraft may provide us, we procured two transom cutouts from Sunset Boat Company, Phoenix, Arizona. The Sunset is an offshore fisherman style watercraft which comes in 18 and 20 foot lengths with either inboard or outboard configurations. It is a popular style patrol boat in Arizona and is used by several agencies. The transom typically is the thickest part of a boat, as it is reinforced with plywood. Our transom was built of 1¾ inches of plywood with a .35 inch layer of fiberglass laminated to it. We shot at it from a distance of ten feet with various calibers to test its resistance to penetration.

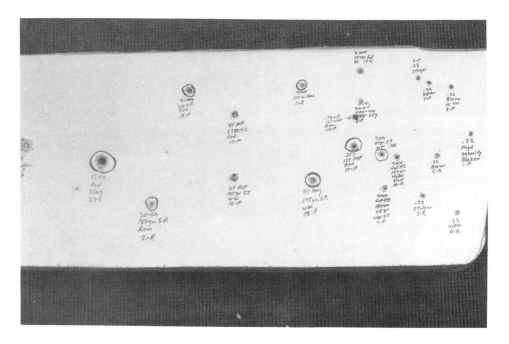

Figure 3. The transom is the thickest part of most boats. W. "Gene" Scott, Rangemaster for the Mesa, Arizona, Police Department, kindly allowed us to use his range for this test. We fired several common calibers against a transom cutout to see how much cover it really provided. Some calibers penetrated the transom.

Ammunition types included .22 caliber (standard velocity, high velocity and super velocity in both pistol and rifle), 9mm Luger (115 gr. FMJ, 115 gr. JHP, 147 gr. JHP in 4″ barrel auto pistol only), .38+P (125 gr. JHP, revolver with 4″ barrel), .357 Magnum (125 gr. JHP, revolver with 4″ barrel), .45 ACP (185 gr. JHP, 235 gr. JHP, auto pistol with 4″ barrel), .41 Magnum (175 gr. JHP, 210 gr. SP, revolver with 6″ barrel), .223

Remington (55 gr. FMJ, rifle with 18″ barrel), 30-06 (180 gr. SP, rifle with 24″ barrel), and 12 ga. (Federal slug, Remington 12 pellet #00 buckshot fired from a 20″ "slug" barrel).

We measured penetration to the back of the bullet, assuming that a depth of less than .35 inches would also indicate that the fiberglass hull (.35 inches) may provide some cover.

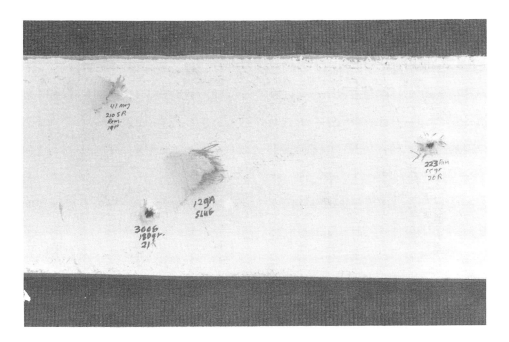

Figure 4. The backside shows exit holes of various bullets which penetrated the transom.

The 12 gauge slug, .41 Magnum, .357 Magnum, .223, and 30-06 all penetrated the transom completely. We can assume that cartridges in this power bracket will overcome a typical boat hull, unless it's specially reinforced by armor.

All other bullets did not penetrate the transom. The following did not penetrate deeper than .35 inches: .22, .38+P, 45 ACP (235 gr. JHP), and the 12 gauge #00 Buck. These would probably not penetrate the boat's hull.

In conclusion, the transom may provide some cover from incoming handgun rounds but not from rifles. You must, however, consider other factors, as most boats do not have just a transom. The engine will provide excellent cover, as will multiple layers of plywood, such as the splash well. You'll also find that equipment and engine covers, seat backs, storage boxes, gas tanks, batteries, etc., will slow incoming rounds.

Your hull provides concealment, if you can avoid showing your silhouette above the gunnel. This can be very difficult, as body bulk varies and some boats have low gunnels.

Figure 5. This Maricopa County Sheriff's Deputy demonstrates one way to use the bow for cover.

This points up the importance of body armor. A vest doesn't protect much body area, and one light enough to wear comfortably won't stop heavy-caliber bullets. Still, you must decide whether partial protection worn all the time is better, or worse, than full protection that's too heavy to wear.

If you find yourself under attack, you must use as much cover and concealment as possible. One tactical drawback is the lack of cover and concealment in most patrol watercraft. Suspects can see you approaching from a distance, nullifying the element of surprise. A smuggler, poacher or other suspect can prepare himself if he intends to resist, and an apparently routine stop can deteriorate into a deadly encounter. You must be prepared to take appropriate countermeasures, including seeking cover and concealment.

Figure 6. This is another technique for maximizing cover. If under attack, use as much cover as you can. Practice taking cover from various areas on your boat, and shoot from these positions during practice sessions. You won't have time to practice when it's for real.

Returning Hostile Fire

You should open fire in a situation in which your action will save your life or someone else's. As a police officer, however, you operate under a severe limitation that a suspect does not: you're responsible for every round you fire. You must be aware of uninvolved subjects in the area and you must be aware of your background. Bullets may skip for hundreds of yards over the water. During close-in attacks, quick and accurate shooting is a must, as you must stop the attacker before you or someone else are hurt.

Think about it. Realize ahead of time that you might be shot. Accept it mentally and you'll find that this mental preparation will allow your mind to react to an attack rather than be occupied with the "Oh Shit" panic response. If you wind up being shot, keep on fighting. Never give up. The will to survive is very powerful, and your positive attitude can make a difference between surviving and perishing. Understanding this in advance avoids taxing your mental processes and slowing your response, which increases your lag time.

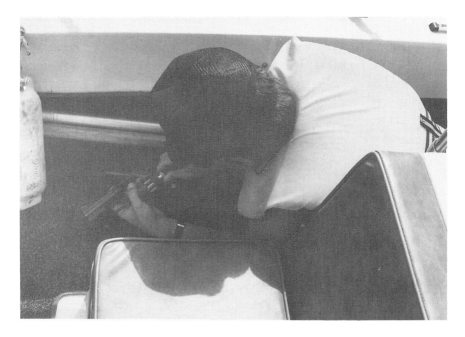

Figure 7. You must also be able to reload while behind cover. With most of his body below the gunnel, this officer reloads his revolver.

You should also be mentally prepared to take another's life to save your own or someone else's. If you can't convince yourself that you can use deadly force to save your life or another's, turn in your badge and find another job. It's not fair to your fellow officers nor your family for you to be mentally handicapped when faced with a deadly force decision.

Your decision to use deadly force should be made well ahead of time. When the attack occurs, your mind needs to be free to deal with the threat and your practiced response to it. Remember, a positive mental attitude is the centerpiece of survival. Skill and confidence in your ability, equipment, and mission will overcome panic, thus giving you precious seconds to employ appropriate countermeasures.

If you are on the water and in contact with a suspect who employs a firearm or knife against you, you must react quickly and do something to distract the attacker. If he decides to attack first, he is taking the initiative, and to stand flat-footed and try to outdraw him is a poor tactic.

"Do the unexpected" is the advice Jerry Scott, of the Ohio Division of Wildlife, offers his students. When a suspect assaults you, react and react quickly. If you've prepared for it through training, practice and mental preparation, you have the advantage. Under stress, your training and practice take over.

If you are in control of the helm, perhaps a ram or sideswipe will throw him off balance long enough to give you an advantage. If the attacker is up close, you should do something to "short-circuit" his intentions. Scream, bat his weapon away, poke him in the eyes, or throw your ticket book in his face. Do something, anything that will throw him off and gain you a split-second's time. This slight edge may let you survive.

A common error when firing from a watercraft is to use the gunnel or other part of the boat as a rest. The boat is moving constantly, rolling in the waves and even in its own wake. By using it as a rest, you're making your firearm a part of the boat. This conducts the boat's motion directly to your firearm and destroys accuracy. To avoid this problem, hold your firearm, forearms and hands a few inches above your cover. Let your arms move up and down in order to keep a steady hold on your target. This technique applies to the handgun, shotgun, and rifle.

Ambushes: Escape and Countermeasures

Officers should be alert to the possibility of ambushes, because though the frequency of this type of attack is low, an ambush can be very dangerous. The assailant takes advantage of surprise and usually launches a deadly attack. Ambushes can happen at anytime. An Arizona officer came under rifle fire when patrolling near a large camp. A suspect shot an Iowa officer in the back with a .22 rifle he had in his boat after the officer had written him a citation and was leaving the scene.

There are many ways to react correctly to an ambush and each has its merit. By contrast, there is only one absolutely wrong way to react and that is to remain still and do nothing. If you stay still, mouth open, and swivel your head looking for the source of the shots, you'll provide your assailant with a sitting duck for a target. Whatever you do, do something!

One type of response is to keep moving. Don't ever offer an ambusher a sitting target. Creating distance between you and the attacker reduces his chances of hitting you. Leaving the scene both deprives your attacker of his target and allows you to request assistance. You may choose to leave the kill zone as quickly as you can or you may zigzag to spoil his aim. Remember that hitting a moving target is easier if the target is coming straight in or moving directly away. Targets moving at 90 degrees require

Figure 8. Keep your gun hands off the gunnel so as to avoid disturbing your aim. Let your hands move independently of the boat's motion.

the most deflection, or lead, and are harder to hit. Targets that change direction rapidly make it hard to anticipate their movements.

While leaving the kill zone, try to take whatever cover or concealment is available and move across the line of fire as rapidly as possible. If possible, place some object between you and your attacker. Moving your boat around a point, or using rocks, trees, or brush to block your attacker's vision, will gain you valuable time to increase the range and make hits less likely.

The most important thing is to keep moving. This is probably the better way to cope with an ambush if you don't know the source of the gunfire aimed at you.

Another basic technique for coping with an ambush is to take cover and return fire. Returning fire is effective if you can see your target and have a reasonable chance of hitting or coming near it. Obviously, taking cover and/or concealment will deny the ambusher a target. If you find his location, returning fire will disable him or drive him to cover himself, thereby impairing his aim. Remember that most sidearms can deliver reasonably accurate fire out to 100 yards. A few near-misses may cause an ambusher to seek cover or break off the attack.

Bill Jordan, formerly of the U. S. Border Patrol, tells of an officer who found himself under fire from a suspect 200 yards away and armed with a rifle. This officer returned fire with his revolver, getting three hits which dissuaded the attacker from continuing the fight. This is an exceptional case, but you ought to keep it in mind if you're ever in a similar situation.[1]

In some situations, trying to escape over water will place you in greater danger. If close to shore, you may decide that you have a better chance seeking cover ashore. If you power your boat onto shore and abandon it, take your portable radio, shoulder weapon, and ammunition. If you take your attacker by surprise, you'll have a chance to seek a defensible position ashore, preferably with your back to a solid object and a good view of all approach routes.

The last option, if you come under accurate fire and there are no other choices left, is to bail out. You can go overboard and use your boat and the water as cover. Water is very dense, and only a few inches will stop most handgun bullets. Navy tests conducted during World War II showed that about three feet of water would stop .30-caliber aircraft machine-gun fire and protect a downed pilot from being strafed by an enemy.

If you go into the water, you'll be glad to know that your sidearm will still shoot. For best results, drain the water from the barrel before firing. With a revolver, use a wrist snap to drain the water out of the barrel. The barrel-cylinder gap will drain the water if you hold the firearm vertically. With an auto pistol, shaking the firearm barrel down will drain the water if the bore is large. If in doubt, pull the slide back partway. In the urgency of the moment, you may even inadvertently eject a live round, but this is better than having an inoperative sidearm.

NOTES

1. Jordan, William, *No Second Place Winner*, 1965, pp. 105–106.

PART III. WATERCRAFT PATROL EQUIPMENT

Chapter 20

OFFICER ITEMS

In this chapter, we'll discuss some items which you should procure for personal use, to survive on watercraft patrol and to make your work more comfortable and effective. Some departments are generous with issued equipment, but you can't depend on your agency to supply every item you may need. You may leave personal items aboard your patrol craft or you may carry them with you in some type of duffel bag. You'll need many of the following items:

Personal Gear

Safety Goggles

If your patrol boat lacks a windshield and does not provide you with full facial protection, you should obtain good quality clear-lens goggles. The advantage of these over glasses is that they also provide protection on the sides of your eyes. Always wear these while performing night work, when you need both good visibility and eye protection.

Sunglasses

Studies have shown that constant exposure to ultraviolet radiation may lead to cataract formation. As a water patrol officer, your eyes are exposed to intense doses of UV, both directly from the sun and that reflected from the water. Even if your eyes are in shade from a boat top or hat, UV reflections from the water still affect them. Doctors recommend the darkest lens you can tolerate for best protection. Another recommendation is to have the lenses treated with 100% UV protection. You may also have this treatment applied to clear glasses if you don't like to wear sunglasses. The drawback of dark glasses is that of public image. Some people feel threatened when they cannot see another's eyes. You should keep this in mind and remove your glasses while speaking with the public. However, in the Southwest, so many people wear sunglasses that this is not a serious problem. It's still good practice to avoid the "mirror" glasses. An important tactical tip is that if you don't need glasses for vision, you should always remove them if you encounter a hostile situation. If you need visual correction, employ a safety strap to ensure that your glasses won't fall off from shock or movement. This would leave you impaired during a dangerous encounter. A safety strap may also prevent you from losing a good pair of glasses overboard.

Sunblock

This is a "must" for most water officers. UV also affects your skin. The higher the protection number on the lotion, the higher the degree of protection. Doctors recommend that you wear the highest level you can find. You should find a type that is also water resistant. Certain types of complexions are extremely sensitive to sunburn and, if yours is of this type, sun-blocking lotion is essential. As well as being painful, sunburn can cause skin cancer. This is a delayed and cumulative effect and can occur years after exposure. In Arizona, game rangers have one of the highest rates of skin cancer among state employees. State risk management personnel have given game and fish officers classes on the prevention of skin cancer. All officers are now issued sunblock with a rating of 44. Another precaution is that patrol boats all have Bimini tops to provide shade.

Lip Protection

Using a good grade of lip ointment will prevent chapped, cracked and split lips, caused by constant exposure to the elements.

Canteen

You should carry enough drinking water to last your shift, and drink it before you feel thirsty. Fluid replenishment is important while on patrol in order to prevent dehydration.

If you don't like the taste of plain water, carry a cooler full of soft drinks, although this is both more bulky and more expensive. Also note that heavily sugared drinks aren't as thirst-quenching as low-calorie drinks or plain water.

Non-Slip Shoes or Boots

Your footwear must have non-slip soles. If you are doing shore work, you may want to purchase a pair of canvas boots, which provide ankle protection. These should be of quick-drying material and should be high enough to provide good foot and ankle protection.

Head Protection

Head covering is important, because your exposed head can lose up to 50 percent of your body heat. In hot climates, headgear will protect your head from sunburn and heat effects, as well as shade your eyes.

Gloves

Gloves are a must if you handle lines. In cold climates, they also prevent heat loss. If handling wet items in colder climes, you'll need waterproof gloves for full protection.

Safety Equipment

Personal PFD

Procure a PFD that fits you and is within your uniform requirements. Put agency ID, such as a badge and name patch, on it and wear it. Select the type applicable to the water in which you work.

Rain Gear

You should have a set of good rain gear. A jacket with a hood and a pair of rain pants will keep you dry in rain squalls or high winds.

Float Coat

This is a Type III PFD which looks like a coat. Obtain the type with an internal groin protector which is deployed in the water. It also has a built-in hood. This is a good item to have and serves quite well as a warm coat. Keep your personal PFD, rain gear and float coat with you in a duffel bag and take it with you to each assignment, instead of depending on the boat's on-board supplies.

Survival Suit

This can be crucial if you work in a climate in which water and air temperatures promote hypothermia. Survival suits are also known as "exposure suits," and the degree of protection varies with climate. Some have built-in hoods and many have inflating collars, which you can blow up by mouth. Your agency should issue you a well-fitting survival suit as a matter of policy. Attach your agency ID and wear your gun belt on the outside.

Strobe Light

This is essential during night operations. Always fasten your strobe to your PFD while on night patrol. Some strobes become activated upon contact with water. Strobes should also have a manually operated switch and have a lens which will not concentrate the beam.

Cyalume Light Sticks

These chemical lights are handy to have as emergency locator lights at night. Because they are cold lights, they produce no flame and emit no heat. Some emergency responders use these in areas where there is danger of explosion from gas or volatile fuels.

Personal Signal Kit

A good signal kit contains a couple of aerial flares, a signal mirror, a smoke grenade, and a whistle. Most kits come in a small package that fits handily in a coat pocket, glove box, or first-aid kit. In remote areas, signaling devices will greatly assist a support helicopter in locating your position.

Whistle

These noisemakers are useful, because a whistle will carry over longer distances than a yell and takes less energy to project.

Law Enforcement Equipment

Briefcase or Patrol Case

This carries your regulation book, extra citations, seizure tags, evidence receipts, spare batteries, spare pens, etc. You must carry extra items necessary to complete all the paperwork required to finish your job and other small items which occasionally become necessary. A briefcase, attache case, or pursuit case is a convenient device to carry such items.

Evidence Kit

This serves to help collect, identify and store evidence required for successful prosecution. A compact evidence kit should contain: gauze

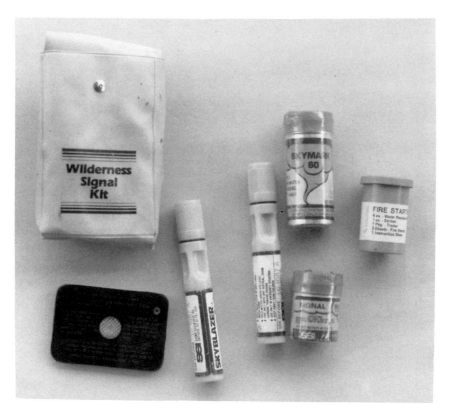

Figure 1. A small signal kit is easy to carry and stow aboard your vessel. It may be invaluable when trying to mark your location for assistance.

pads for blood samples, various sizes of envelopes, plastic and paper bags for evidence storage, marking pens, grease pencils, permanent markers, marking awl, seizure tags, evidence tags, a small camera and flash, tape measure, cotton swabs, tape for marking and sealing, pipe cleaners for attaching tags and securing items, rubber gloves, fingerprint dusting powder, fingerprint brush, lifting tape, and fingerprint record cards. Every officer should assemble his own evidence kit, instead of buying one, because most kits on the market are overpriced. Carrying loose items in an ammo box isn't as elegant as having a leather case with built-in loops, but the ammo box is watertight.

Accident Investigation Kit

If you do accident investigations, a kit will facilitate evidence collection. Some items to include are: boating accident investigation forms, investi-

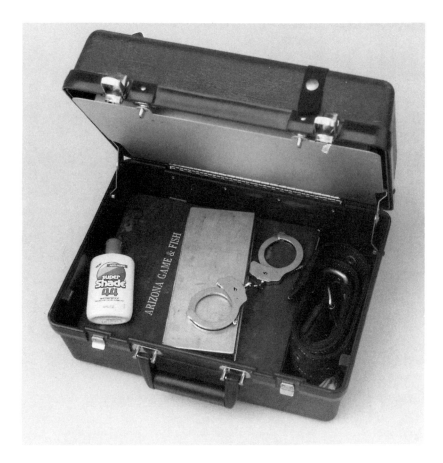

Figure 2. This patrol case carries paperwork and equipment essential to modern police work. An extra set of handcuffs and a transport belt easily fit into the case.

gative cue cards, tape measure, camera (with flash, extra film and batteries), work clothes or coveralls (to protect uniform), tape recorder, flashlight, tools, charts, thermometer, an inspection mirror, and appropriate drawing templates such as "Bear-Aide."

Extra Handcuffs

Usually, you find bad guys in pairs or groups. If you have only a single set of cuffs, you'll quickly appreciate the need for extras, whether metal or flexible nylon. These are similar to electricians' "tie wraps" and are fairly inexpensive. However, some suspects have been known to "burn" their way loose using shoe laces, which is why you should use those with wire molded into them.

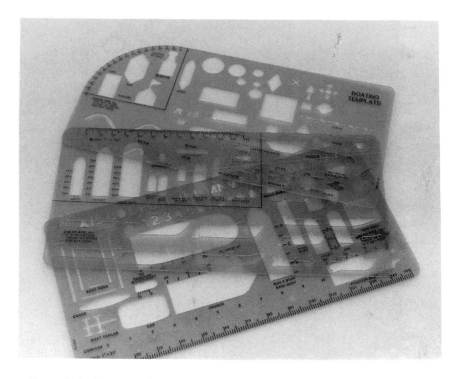

Figure 3. Accident templates take up little room but help sketch the accident scene.

Security Strap

This simple device, also known as a "dog leash," consists of a three-foot length of ¼″ line with a snap attached to one end and a non-closing loop on the other. It's used to "hog-tie" violent handcuffed suspects. To do this, you pass the snap through the loop, thus forming a snare, which you place over the suspect's feet before fastening the snap to the handcuffs in back. This pulls the feet up near the hands and effectively prevents further kicking and violent struggles. With a small suspect, you'll have to shorten the strap by looping it around several times. Make sure the snap is far from his hands. These are available commercially but are easily made if you want to save a couple of bucks. The dog leash takes up little space but is worth its weight in gold when you're trying to control a resisting suspect on board a watercraft.

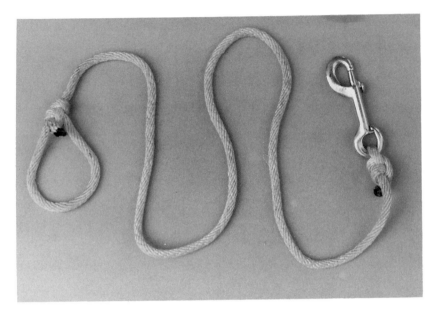

Figure 4. A security strap is inexpensive to make and gives you an easy way to control a violent suspect.

Transport Belt/Chain

This is made from leather, nylon, or metal chain and it secures a suspect's cuffed hands in front of him. The transport belt is handy when transporting prisoners from one facility to another. However, a lone officer should never try to use one. Watercraft officers may occasionally use one to secure a non-violent suspect to transport him a long distance over water. For your safety, you're better off leaving the suspect's hands cuffed and double-locked behind his back.

Citation Book and Clipboard

Citations are best kept inside a hard case to both protect the citations and provide a hard writing surface. Small citation books are hard to handle on a bouncing boat, and some officers have fastened a cover to a legal-sized clipboard, finding this easier to handle. Others use a small clipboard, with only one citation at a time. When you issue citations, you should keep the completed copies in a separate dry-storage container, such as a plastic bag or sandwich box. You don't want an irate subject throwing your court originals into the drink!

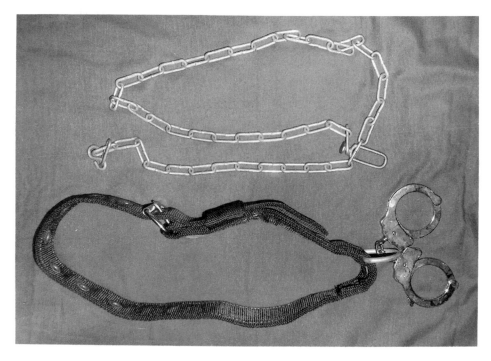

Figure 5. Transport belts and chains provide extra security for the officer who must transport prisoners over long distances.

Clip-On Pen Light

This small goose-necked clip-on light is very handy for writing at night. Clipped onto your shirt, PFD, or ticket book, it frees both hands for writing citations. Its relatively small field of illumination avoids backlighting you and from impairing your night vision. Its beam is not nearly as bright as that from a regular flashlight. You can also paint the bulb red, further protecting your night vision.

Large Flashlight (3 to 5 "D" Cells)

These large flashlights serve two purposes: providing a bright light and as a straight baton in an assault. Most officers replace the regular bulb with a quartz-halogen or krypton bulb in order to increase light output.

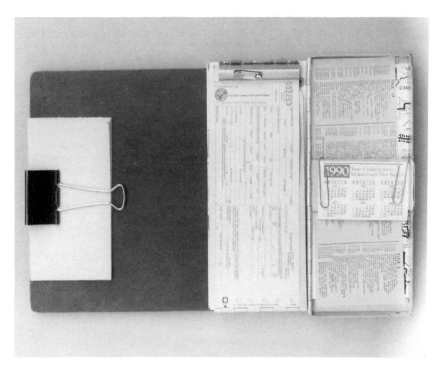

Figure 6. A hard aluminum citation book holder fastened to a legal-sized clipboard provides a large and portable writing surface. It can also be used as a defensive weapon to "short circuit" an attacker. A jab to the face or throat will surprise him and give you an advantage.

Mini-Light

A recent addition to officers' field equipment, these small lights are easy to carry on the gunbelt or in a pocket. They are handy for boarding inspections, when a little extra light is needed to check an HIN or other equipment numbers. They are useful to inspect compartments, instead of reaching in with your hand. They can also serve as an improvised Kubotan and in suspect searches. John Peters, defensive tactics instructor, points out in both his books and videotapes that probing a suspect's pockets with a mini-flashlight is safer than inserting the hand, and it's preferable to use a flashlight when searching females.[1]

Binoculars

Very handy for all patrol work, a good pair will last an entire career. These are a must for proper officer tactics. They will allow you to check a boat, subject or camp before you approach. A special point is that it's possible to lose binoculars overboard. One model that gives good quality, with moderate price, is the rubber-armored, camouflage color, Bushnell Ensign compact, 7×25, Model 13-7206.

Camera

Good pictures will document evidence and tie the crime or accident scene together. If a good camera is not available, the inexpensive kinds using size 110 film and expendable flash attachments will yield acceptable prints, if used within their limitations. They're inexpensive enough to be a component of evidence and accident investigation kits.

Tape Recorder

Small pocket-size tape recorders make recording accident scene information easier. Observations and interviews can be directly recorded for later transcribing. Some officers make sure conversations with drunken, hostile, or felony suspects are on tape and available for court use, or in case of future problems.

Portable Radio

This is important for communicating with your partner if you become separated. If your communication system is good, you'll be able to communicate with land units, other agencies and your dispatcher.

Baton, (Straight, Side Handle, Collapsible, Kubotan)

Whatever intermediate impact weapon you select, become proficient with it. Each has its benefits and drawbacks. An increasingly popular one for watercraft officers is the A.S.P. collapsible baton, because it can be carried on the gun belt with little effort. It's lightweight, can be deployed quickly, and doesn't become entangled between your legs as do the longer straight and side handle models. The collapsible baton does double duty. Collapsed, you can use it as a judo stick or Kubotan. Extended, you can use straight baton techniques.

One-Handed Knife

A personal knife carried on your person or gun belt is probably more useful than any other piece of equipment. Most officers carry the large folding varieties in a pouch on their gun belts. Unfortunately, most of these require two hands to open. If, for some reason, you are unable to use one of your hands, you'll quickly find it impossible to use your knife.

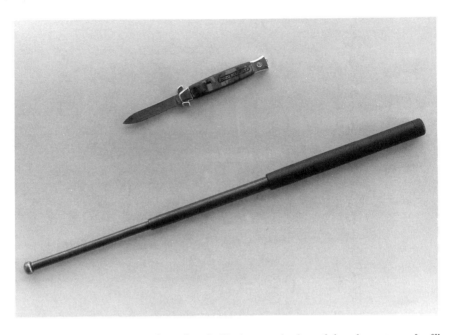

Figure 7. Collapsible batons and one-handed knives are both useful to the watercraft officer.

This is why officers need a knife that they can open and use with only one hand. There are several folding varieties with a tab on the blade that allow one-handed opening. There are also spring-loaded knives that instantly deploy with one-handed operation. These are known as "auto-knives" and are easy to use with either hand.

Chemical Weapons

Many officers don't like using CS or CN aerosols, feeling that the only person gas will always reliably affect is themselves. A new product, "CAP–STUN," uses a pepper solution, and the maker states that it's more effective and has a lower danger level than CS or CN.[2] Whichever type you use, you should know its limitations, practice its use, and have it always available. Some agencies now use gas grenades in felony boating stops. The technique has merit but with an important reservation. Gas generators should be of the non-pyrotechnic type, as boats contain a great deal of flammable material.

Body Armor

This is a vital item of survival gear. Personal soft armor has saved hundreds of police officers' lives and may even save yours someday. Threat level of your armor should match what you expect to encounter. At least, it must stop the bullets in your sidearm, because that firearm will be in every one of your contacts. FBI statistics show that 20 percent of officers killed each year are killed with their own guns. Even one officer killed is too many, especially if that one killed is you!

For most officers, the recommendation is to wear armor no heavier than Threat Level II. The problem with armor is that bulk and weight increase with the protection level. Excessively heavy and bulky armor is also warmer than lighter grades, increasing your discomfort, and you may be tempted to leave it behind. A vest designed to stop a .41 Magnum won't do you any good if it's at home while a suspect shoots you with a rimfire .22. This is why many believe that proper fit and comfort are more important than protection level.

Many watercraft officers feel that armor will weigh them down if they go into the water. To test this, the authors placed modern Threat Level II armor (not the type encased in plastic) in water for over an hour. At the end, it was still floating. The authors also tested a set of old body armor by wearing it in water. The old style was not watertight, nor impregnated with water-repellent chemical. The vest floated for about 20 minutes, aided by an air pocket that had formed. As this dissipated, buoyancy gradually became neutral and then slightly negative. It did not pull the wearer down, but when removed, it slowly sank to the bottom of the pool.

If you fall overboard wearing soft body armor, without metal or ceramic inserts, it won't pull you down at first and it will even provide slight initial buoyancy. Your gun belt, with several pounds of metal, is a greater danger.

Most body armor panels are treated with a chemical water repellent, because untreated fabrics lose some resistance to penetration when soaking wet. However, normal perspiration isn't enough to affect ballistic resistance noticeably. Even if your vest is completely soaked, it will come back to normal performance when dry.[3]

We can't recommend body armor with panels encased in a plastic envelope to keep it bone-dry. This type of waterproofing also blocks perspiration, which makes it very uncomfortable to wear. As we've seen, ballistic protection doesn't deteriorate noticeably with small amounts of moisture, which makes total waterproofing unnecessary.

You may want to conduct your own tests on body armor on which you stake your life. Second Chance, a major manufacturer, will provide test samples of armor to officers, and we suggest that you conduct your own experiments and draw your own conclusions.

Stun Gun

A recent arrival on the police market, this small hand-held device is no bigger than a portable radio. Powered by a 9-volt battery, the stun gun's two electrodes send a high-voltage current into the suspect's body on contact. The shock and pain will temporarily disable most suspects, making them easier to handle and arrest. A major drawback is that you must get within the suspect's danger zone and hold the electrodes against him for several seconds. Many agencies are starting to issue these, and if your patrol beat involves much close-in work with assaultive suspects, you should consider carrying one of these intermediate-force weapons.

We have to add other warnings here. At their introduction, stun guns were hyped by advertisers and their effectiveness exaggerated. They do work but not on everyone. They also have certain dangers. If you or your suspect are wet when you trigger one, you might get the voltage back through your body. Another problem is sparking. Never use a stun gun around flammable vapors, as tests have shown that the sparks these produce will ignite gasoline, benzene, and other flammables.

Backup Gun

Besides your regular sidearm, you should have, on or near your person, a second gun or a backup gun. These terms are not synonymous. The "second gun" is a spare to save you time in reloading. The "backup" is in case your service firearm jams or a suspect disarms you. The main point regarding second or backup guns is that they should always be of the same type and caliber as your service gun. This avoids fumbling and unfamiliarity in bringing the second gun into operation and allows using the same ammunition.

Riot Gun with Magazine Extender

This firearm should be mandatory on every watercraft. You'll be glad you have one handy during felony arrests, because a shotgun can provide decisive firepower. You may be required to go ashore as a first response unit or to back up another unit responding to a felony. A long gun is indispensable for this role. An extender enhances the limited magazine capacity of most riot guns. This give you at least three extra rounds. Also attach a sling, for easy carry, and to allow you to "sling" your shotgun in case you need both hands. A slug barrel with rifle sights is desirable. Current shotgun combat philosophy recommends a "ghost ring" rear sight rather than the more conventional open sights, but choose the one best for your eyes. Either way, rifle sights give you good accuracy with slug rounds and improve the efficiency of this tool. Also remember other uses for a shotgun, such as a platform for launching gas grenades.

Police Rifle

A carbine or light rifle in .223 caliber is fast becoming the long gun of choice for many officers because of long range, high fire rate, and long-distance accuracy. Consider a rifle's suitability for your current assignment. If your agency doesn't issue rifles but you feel that one will enhance your survival prospects, buy your own.

Figure 8. The Ruger Mini-14 is a favorite light rifle with many officers. The Choate Stock Extender makes the buttstock fit adult dimensions. Easy to store and use, it provides accurate firepower.

Spare Ammo Container

You need to provide yourself with an easily carried and sealed ammo carrier for dry storage. Extra ammo allows you to change the rounds in your firearm in case of water immersion. For best efficiency, carry your spare ammo in spare magazines, speedloaders, shotshell belts, etc., rather than in original boxes. This avoids the delay from loading boxed ammo into a magazine in an urgent situation.

Gun Belt

Your gun belt is the primary carrier for your law enforcement equipment. Purchasing cheap duty gear is false economy because it will fail you under stress and won't last as long as good quality gear. Most officers use the gun belt to carry the sidearm, spare ammo carriers, knife, handcuffs, baton holder, portable radio holder, chemical weapon, mini-flashlight holder, flashlight ring, keys, etc. Avoid overloading your belt, because you'll be uncomfortable and it may restrict your free movement. Your selection of a holster is critical, and you should choose one that holds your sidearm securely and gives you immediate control over it in case of an attempted "snatch." The holster should fit flat against your body and be secured with a retention device. You should be able to draw easily from it, but an alternative retention device (screw, welt, etc.) should keep the sidearm in the holster if turned upside down when unsnapped.

Ballistic Nylon vs. Leather

Although leather gear is traditional among police, many SWAT teams have chosen nylon gear because the new material fits their needs better than leather. Whether you choose Cordura or ballistic nylon, you'll find that the synthetic is less vulnerable to water damage than leather. Both are less expensive, lighter, and they come in non-reflective finishes. As nylon holsters have little metal and no chrome or brass fixtures, they're more durable and easier to maintain. There are no police leather items without nylon counterparts. For watercraft use, a major advantage is that nylon dries more quickly and is easier to maintain than leather when exposed to constant humidity. Many watercraft patrol agencies now allow officers to use nylon instead of leather. If your unit doesn't, perhaps you should try to persuade your superiors to change policy.

NOTES

1. Peters, John G. Jr., *Defensive Tactics With Flashlights.* videotape, Albuquerque, New Mexico, 1988.
2. *POLICE,* Vol. 14, Number 3, March, 1990, p. 16.
3. *Law Enforcement & Military Body Armor Selection Guide,* Personal Protective Armor Association, April, 1990.

Chapter 21

WATERCRAFT RIGGING

Your patrol watercraft should be rigged to conform to local laws, agency policies and personal needs. Many patrol boats are modified civilian pleasure craft, as most agencies' budgets don't allow custom-designed and rigged patrol boats. As a result, they're usually rigged in a central motor pool. If this is the case with your agency, you may need additional rigging to suit your needs. The following list may not include all the items that you need, but it serves as a basic guideline for rigging your watercraft, trailer and accessories.

Trailer Rigging

Trailer

Watercraft trailers should be designed to match the hull of your patrol boat and balanced so that no more than 7 percent of the total weight is on the trailer tongue. Heavy-duty construction, including a protective coating, is a must. Many trailers are painted, but others are galvanized. All should have fenders, stop, turn and license plate lights, and dual welded safety chains with hooks. Most manufacturers provide "surge" brakes, which activate when the boat and trailer are pushed forward during a stop. This is an excellent safety feature but can be frustrating when trying to back a heavy boat uphill. Another requirement is a safety system to activate the brakes if the trailer becomes separated from the towing vehicle. You should install anti-slip material (either tape or paint) on all parts of the trailer where you step. Wet metal, especially if painted, can be quite slick and cause a fall. Some officers have footpads welded to their trailers in places where the trailer does not provide safe footing. This provides a safe flat place to step when climbing between the trailer tongue and the boat.

Figure 1. A watercraft trailer takes much abuse. It must be constructed of materials that will provide years of safe service.

Bow Safety Chain and Snap

A stout chain from your trailer to the bow eye of your boat prevents losing your boat if the bow cable breaks. The snap makes it easy to hook and unhook the chain.

Bow Winch

A heavy-duty winch is necessary to pull your boat into proper position on the trailer when loading. Some agencies have installed electric bow winches, using the towing vehicle's electrical system, which greatly assists loading large vessels. A bi-directional ratchet locks the cable.

Bow Cable and Snap

The bow winch should be fitted with a high quality cable or nylon strap, long enough for easy loading of the boat. Some officers drive the boat onto the trailer, while others use the bow cable to pull the boat. The cable and winch must be of sufficient power and durability to be able to handle hundreds of loadings. Regularly inspect the cable or strap for fraying and replace any defective items immediately. We do not recommend the use of rope substitutes for cable. Rope frays too quickly and isn't as durable. The bow cable holds the boat securely on the trailer during transport. If you have a fiberglass boat, you should reduce the tension on the cable while the boat is in storage in order to relieve the strain on the bow eye and on the hull where it rests on the trailer bunks or rollers. Always check the security of your bow cable and bow chain before towing your boat.

Transom Tie-Downs

These straps or chains secure the stern of the boat to the trailer, attaching the two stern tow eyes to the respective sides of the trailer. If you tow a boat over rough roads or hit a bump, these keep the rear of the boat from bouncing into the air, reducing wear and tear on your hull and trailer rollers or bunks.

Trailer Rollers or Bunks

The weight of the hull rests on rollers or bunks. Rollers are rubber cylinders and bunks are wooden planks usually covered with carpet. Rollers are only to protect the hull from damage by the trailer on steep ramps and to guide the hull onto proper position on the bunks. The hull's weight should rest on the bunks, because the roller's small contact area concentrates the weight of the boat on several small spots on the hull. This causes uneven stress on the hull, which is designed to evenly distribute the weight over water and not in concentrated areas.

Trailer Side Rails

Two of these padded rails, attached on either side of the trailer, contact the boat about halfway up the side of the hull. They aid in loading the boat by centering the hull on the trailer and are indispensable when loading in current, wind, or darkness.

Engine Support

This device, known as a "transom saver," allows the lower unit to rest on a "Y"-shaped fork attached to the trailer. These transfer the engine's weight to the trailer, thus taking weight off the transom while in tow or storage. The engine support also allows the engine to sit at a lower angle than when resting on the normal up-position tabs. You should never tow or store your watercraft with the engine held up solely by the hydraulic lift system, as this places stress on your power tilt system and increases the chance of failure.

Bearing Buddies

Each time you launch your boat, you submerge your trailer's axles and water enters to rust your wheel hubs. "Bearing buddies" facilitate routine maintenance and reduce potential accidents, as they allow adding grease when leaving the water. This prevents bearing rust and frozen wheels. Your trailer should have a hand-held grease gun loaded with marine wheel bearing grease, not regular vehicle grease. A bearing buddy bra slipped over the end of the buddy will keep loose grease from fouling up your hull, trailer, and wheels.

Spare Tire

Make sure your spare matches the wheels and tires on your trailer. Often, maintenance shop employees mismatch them. Check tires often for inflation and tread separation. In the Southwest, they can dry out and crack with prolonged exposure to the sun. Regular spraying with "Armor-All" or a similar product reduces cracks caused by atmospheric ozone.

Spare Tire Lock

Watercraft trailer spares are easily accessible for theft. A tire lock, even a chain and padlock, will prevent most thefts.

Trailer Jack

It's easy to forget this item until you need it. Trailers sit lower to the ground, and many vehicle jacks will not fit the gap. Check yours now, and if it doesn't work, get one that does. The bottle type hydraulic jack works quite well, is inexpensive, and easy to use.

Trailer Tongue Jack

Most employee back injuries I have investigated came from wrestling trailers onto vehicle hitches. Make sure your trailer has a sturdy tongue jack. Jack wheels make aligning hitch and ball a little easier. Also check your jack type. Some have wheels designed to come off, but others are permanently mounted. Before towing, make sure the jack is in the correct position.

Mooring, Trailering Cover

A boat cover that fits well protects your watercraft and its components from the elements. It also provides some security for your equipment when you are unable to keep it under observation. Your cover should fit snugly and tie down tightly on the trailer. You should also be able to leave it on the boat during towing. Many agencies leave their boats on the water between shifts, and a good cover will provide protection for an open boat and its equipment. However, if your boat has an enclosed cabin or a permanent "T" top, a cover may not be practical.

Watercraft Rigging

Fasteners

All items should be securely fastened with stainless steel or chrome bolts, washers and lock nuts. Do not accept items fastened with screws, because these tend to pull out of their holes. Also make sure that there is sufficient backing, such as a large washer or a backup metal plate, to hold the item in place. Each month (or more often as needed) you must check and tighten all bolts and nuts on the boat, because jarring and vibration of a watercraft tend to loosen fasteners, regardless of how well tightened they may be.

Power Trim and Tilt

If you're operating any patrol craft larger than a small outboard, power trim and tilt are mandatory. This system lets you adjust the trim of the craft while under way for peak performance; to raise the engine in shallow water; to raise the engine for trailering; and to raise the engine while in the water for prop and lower unit inspection.

Dual Cable Steering

This safety feature is a must with larger engines. Dual cables provide uninterrupted control if a steering cable breaks. Dual cables also prevent rapid, uncontrollable turns that may eject the operator or passengers.

Central Fuse Panel

Non-metal boats are wired differently from metal ones. Without a metal chassis for a common negative ground, all circuits require two wires. Many manufacturers employ "in-line" fuses. If a fuse blows, it becomes necessary to trace each wire to find and check its in-line fuse. This requires a lot of time, patience and mechanical ability. One way to solve this problem is to have one large fuse panel, which contains about

20 fuses, wired in between the battery and the rest of the equipment. Besides providing an easily accessible panel, there are enough extra spaces to add accessories easily. You install your accessory, connect your positive and negative wires to the new fuse location, insert the appropriate amperage fuse and you're in business.

Dual-Battery System

Marine batteries come in two basic types, the marine "cranking" and the marine "deep cycle." Mistakenly using one type instead of the other can have serious consequences, because each battery type serves a distinct purpose. A cranking battery is designed to provide maximum power for a short time, but a deep-cycle battery provides consistent delivery over a long interval. Cranking batteries are used to start engines, but deep cycles are for the constant drain of operating equipment, such as trolling motors.

We have found that a dual cranking battery system provides for reliable starts and few battery problems. The batteries are wired to a battery switch to allow using both batteries, or either one separately. The switch also has an "off" feature that shuts down your entire system. This is a good anti-theft device as well as a way to eliminate battery drain if you forget to turn off a piece of equipment. The dual switch is wired to let you read the status of each battery on a battery gauge, or charge the batteries individually, as you wish. If you operate a system that needs a deep-cycle battery, such as a trolling motor, you should not have this run through the boat charging system but installed on its own separate system.

Your engine should have the highest amperage alternator available. Patrol boats produce a higher electrical drain due to all the accessories. Engine alternators are not designed to charge deep-cycle batteries, because these need power input over a long period of time, such as a separate system powered through a conventional battery charger and outside electrical source.

External Battery Terminals

Connected to the positive and negative terminals, these externally mounted posts provide a safe access to your battery system for "jumping" other boats. You allow the other boater to hook up the cables to his boat first and then you connect the cables to your external terminal posts. There is no need to crawl into the battery area, with the danger of

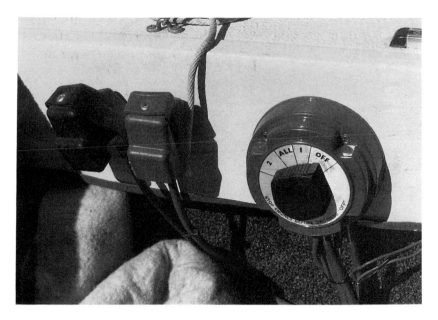

Figure 2. Your boat should be equipped with dual batteries. This type of switch allows you to use both batteries, individually or together.

causing sparks near the explosive battery gases, and the danger of exploding batteries is sharply reduced. Terminals also allow charging batteries overnight by connecting the charger to them, without the inconvenience of placing cables in tight quarters. Some agencies have their jumper cables hard-wired into the battery system with a remote switch for the extra convenience.

Lighted Instruments

All your helm instruments should have built-in lighting. This eliminates the need for external helm lights which destroy your night vision. If possible, have red bulbs installed instead of white.

Battery Status Gauge

As we mentioned while discussing the dual-battery system, this instrument allows you to monitor the status of your cranking batteries.

Engine Tilt Indicator

This gauge is an important part of your power trim and tilt system, as it lets you see the positioning of your lower unit.

Figure 3. External terminals mounted away from the batteries allows for safe and hassle-free battery charging. They also make jump starting other boats much safer.

Cigar Lighter Jack

Whether you smoke or not, this accessory allows the use of a portable boarding or running light (jack light). There are other devices, such as map lights, that also plug into this jack. Some patrol boats have two jacks, to allow both the operator and his partner to have his own light.

Cockpit Lights

On an open boat, these should be mounted low to the deck in order to provide adequate light without backlighting you during night operations. If you have storage areas, these lights will be helpful when looking for equipment at night.

Driving Lights

If the manufacturer of your new boat welcomes suggestions from users and is willing to make design changes, an important addition is to install driving lights in the bow of your craft. These are typically sealed headlights, mounted below the gunnel, to provide forward lighting similar to auto headlamps.

Bilge Pump

This is an absolute must, because there's no other safe way to eliminate bilge water while away from shore. Some pumps have automatic switches, while others use manual switches. An important point in making the choice is that automatic systems may cause operator complacency and you may not discover a malfunctioning bilge system until someone's feet get wet!

Kill Switch

An important safety feature, this device is attached to the operator with a lanyard when working in dangerous waters. If the operator falls overboard, the kill switch shuts off the engine automatically. The kill switch also has some tactical uses. It's a quick way to stop the prop if there is danger of the prop causing damage, because it's faster than turning off the key switch. In case of a fight, a quick pull on the lanyard stops the engine. If you leave the boat in a hurry, you can take the switch with you, preventing theft. However, there are occasional problems with kill switches. If, for example, your boat won't start even if the battery sounds good, check the kill switch. It may have been bumped. They can also become lost, which is why you should always keep an extra switch in your glove box. If yours is lost, stolen, or goes overboard attached to your partner, you won't be able to start the boat without it.

Threaded Bilge Plug

All patrol boats should have threaded bilge plugs, which can only be installed and removed with a wrench. This prevents anyone from sinking your boat while unattended. If your bilge plug is the rubber insert type, get it converted to a threaded style.

Helm Protection

If you operate an open boat, you'll need overhead protection. There are three types or styles of tops. The "T" top is a rigid top, usually made of metal, that is high enough above the cockpit to allow the operator and passengers to walk underneath it. Because its construction is rigid, it also can serve for mounting radar units, blue lights, sirens, PAs, radio antennas and other devices. The Bimini top is of cloth or canvas and it can be stowed when not in use. As it's collapsible, it's not a secure base for equipment. It does provide a great deal of protection to the helm area

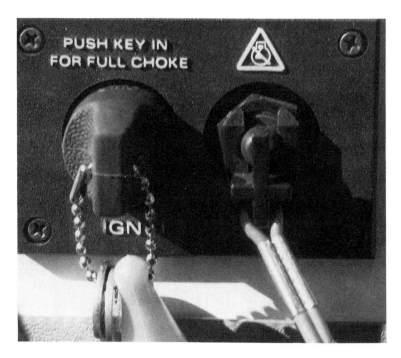

Figure 4. A kill switch is a must. It also serves as an emergency cut-off switch for the engine.

from both sun and rain. The convertible top is usually used in runabout craft and is fastened to both the windshield and stern. Second only to a cabin, this top provides the most protection to an operator and passengers. The drawbacks are that it only allows for seated operation, hampers work, and usually does not allow standing, as well as restricting your vision.

Swim Platforms

Mounted on both sides of the transom, they are out of the way and allow for easy access into the boat from the water.

Boarding Ladder

Permanently attached to the transom, the ladder allows for access to the boat. A ladder's harder to use than a swim platform and doesn't provide secure footing. Without swim platforms or boarding ladders, a large patrol boat is almost impossible to board if you find yourself in the water. It's also difficult or impossible to load an injured person from the water into the boat. The only other choice is to lean over and pull the victim up over the gunnel.

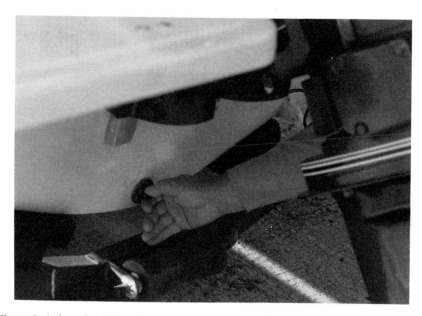

Figure 5. A threaded bilge plug prevents easy removal by vengeful suspects or vandals.

Figure 6. A canvas "Bimini" top protects you from the sun or other adverse weather. On desert lakes, these are vital.

Portable Ladder

These collapsible ladders are stored and quick to deploy when and where needed.

Bow Line and Snap

Used to tie the boat from the bow, the bow line should never be longer than the distance from the bow eye to the prop for obvious reasons. If you haven't checked your bow line's length and it falls into the water while moving, you'll probably foul your prop and be disabled. You should put a snap at each end of the bow line, to allow for quick attachment to the bow, as well as to anchor lines and beach lines.

Anchor Line and Snap

This line is to attach the anchor to the bow line, or bow eye, as well as to tie the patrol boat to shore. In combination with the anchor and chain, it's known as the "rode." The length of the rode is called its "scope." Because anchors work best with horizontal pull, the ideal scope is 7 times the depth of the water. You can get by with a scope of 5 to 1, if the bottom provides enough material for the anchor to dig in for a secure hold. However, you must know your patrol area well enough to estimate the amount of rode necessary for secure anchoring. Larger vessels have sufficient storage for spools of line, but small patrol boats must rely on the experience of the operator to select an appropriate length.

A snap on each end allows quick and easy attachment to the anchor chain or to on-shore anchor points. These are to hold the boat while you are on shore. One good technique is to use the anchor and rode as an on-shore mooring. When responding to a call or emergency ashore, the officer carries the rode, pulls it taut, and drops the anchor on shore. This eliminates the need to spend valuable time looking for a secure fastening point. It also allows you to respond rapidly without concern that your patrol boat might drift away.

Anchor

Anchor selection is critical and depends on the bottom of your patrol area, the size of patrol boat, frequency of use, and prevailing weather conditions. Choice of type will depend on your needs. For soft bottoms, mushroom anchors are sufficient and have good holding power. For its size and weight, the Danforth anchor is probably the best for most patrol functions. This anchor was developed in World War II. It has two long narrow flukes pivoted at the end of a long shank and engages the bottom quickly and handles heavy strain well. Your anchor must be light enough to allow handling by one officer, as well as carrying ashore. A short chain should be connected between the anchor and line, its length determined by bottom conditions. Usually, three to five feet of link chain is enough. A snap on the anchor line provides quick attachment to the chain, allowing easier storage of the line, as well as using the line for several purposes.

Sea Anchor

A cloth/canvas drogue, called a "sea anchor," doesn't really anchor your boat but provides controlled drift. If you operate on a medium-to-large body of water and encounter rough weather conditions with high winds and waves, you must keep your bow into the sea. If your engine fails, you won't be able to keep your bow oriented properly and your patrol craft will be controlled by the weather. You may end up being swamped due to broaching or pitchpoling, and a sea anchor can help you survive this situation. Before deployment, you must make sure that it's attached to your bow. If you don't, you will not be strong enough to attach it once it's out. The drag from the sea anchor will hold your bow into the wind and waves. You will drift with your bow into the wind until you reach shore. If you don't have a sea anchor and find yourself without power in bad weather, you can make one from available materials. Attach anything that will cause drag onto the end of the anchor line. Several life jackets, with a bail bucket securely fastened, may do the trick. DO NOT deploy an anchor. If it grabs on the bottom, it will cause your bow to be pulled down in a wave rather than riding over it. Again, your anchor line with snaps can be rapidly attached to a sea anchor.

Docking Lines

Attached to cleats on the fore and aft and port and starboard areas of your boat, these lines are vital for boardings and for attachment of your patrol boat to docks. They should be permanently attached and between 10 to 14 feet long. Specific length and type of line will vary depending on your patrol area. If you need to perform a felony boarding, you will not have time to remove line from your locker and attach it to both your boat and the suspect's. You need to make sure that your patrol boat has securely attached cleats in the appropriate locations. You should rig these lines yourself to be sure they will meet your needs.

Shot Bags

These are weighted bags tied to your dock lines. If you do a lot of boarding, these will simplify your task. When you throw the bags into the other boat, they will anchor both boats together, except in rough weather. More importantly, shot bags free your hands and attention in a critical situation.

Fenders

Large plastic air-filled cylinders, cloth-filled canvas tubes, or rubber bumpers are all devices used to cushion a boat from damage. They are used between boats or to protect a boat from a sudden impact. You should have at least four fenders. Two fore and two aft on port and starboard sides, and properly adjusted, will prevent most boarding damage. Many officers locate these based on personal choice and operating techniques. Regardless of how you rig and use them, they must be available for immediate use to protect your boat and those of others.

Boat Hook

This is a must for boarding contacts. The hook part of the pole should be padded to prevent damage to the other boat. Each patrol boat should have one or two of these, stout enough to be used to push your boat away from obstructions.

Paddle

One or two of these should be aboard your boat. Make sure they're long enough to reach from the water to a comfortable use position above the gunnel. Large patrol boats are difficult to paddle, especially if the paddles are too short and you have to lean over the gunnel to reach the water. Aluminum ones with plastic paddles usually do not last long enough to be useful. A good paddle or oar can also serve as a push pole. If you have two, you can put your partner to work. As "misery loves company," an extra paddle will help quiet his kibitzing about your engine failure. Two paddles will also help with steerage.

Figure 7. You need a buffer or bumper between your boat and the subject's boat, or a dock. This plastic fender is durable and effective for small-boat boardings.

Tools

Not having enough tools to perform maintenance and repairs can be a very frustrating experience as you drift waiting for assistance. We recommend, as a minimum, the following tools which can be used for most repairs. As a start, you should have the tools needed to tighten your bilge plug and replace a prop. As small items tend to fall overboard, you should always have an extra set of prop washers. If a prop spins off or a piece slips from your grasp, you have lost your ability to make proper repairs, unless you have suitable replacements. Tools should be in a well-built plastic tool box for dry storage. Check them regularly for rust, which can destroy them. The plastic tool box is also a handy place to store the various "extras" you need. Size of tools depends on the size of your engine. A basic list is the following:

10″–12″ slip joint pliers
10″–12″ adjustable (crescent) wrench
Combination box end and open end wrenches
Multi-tipped screwdriver ("4-in-1" style)
Hammer

Electrical tape
Spark plug wrench
"Grease gun"
Tube of marine bearing grease
Set of hex wrenches
One pair of wire cutters

Propellers

These should match your engine and your boat's mission. We recommend three props for each engine. One is on the engine, another is on board as a spare, and the third in the shop being repaired! Prop damage, if your mission includes going ashore or working bank fishermen, is operational overhead. Often, props are cheaper to rebuild than replace. Stainless steel props are more expensive but are preferred by most watercraft officers. As they flex less than aluminum props, their efficiency is better. Consequently, their top end speed is greater, the craft goes on plane more quickly, and the props suffer less damage due to their strength.

Extras

You should have "extras" of the following to replace lost or inoperable items. These may vary depending on the size of your patrol boat and include bilge plugs, a spare gas can, engine oil, gas line, gas line pump bulb, fuses, kill switch and lanyard, trailer light bulbs (clearance, license plate, brake and turn), navigational light bulbs, prop washers, thrust washers, prop nuts, cotter keys or lock washers, stainless steel nuts, bolts and washers, spark plugs, a set of boat keys with key float, a fuel filter, an extra water separator filter, and a hundred feet of extra line.

Safety Equipment

Fire Extinguishers

Fire extinguishers must be U.S. Coast Guard approved Marine Type B. This means they are designed to put out fires from flammable liquids. In addition to your state-required extinguishers, we recommend a minimum of two five-pound, one 10-pound and one 20-pound extinguisher per patrol boat. The actual need will vary, depending upon the size of your vessel. You should place extinguishers strategically around your patrol boat to be easily accessible to you and your partner. The type with the visual gauge allows you to quickly inspect its status. Your agency should have annual fire extinguisher inspections. If yours does, make sure your extinguishers all get inspected and their tags updated. Recharge or replace any deficient ones. You should keep them mounted in heavy-duty brackets, in areas away from moisture. If your boat has an enclosed engine compartment, consider an automatic extinguisher system using Halon gas. These provide effective on-board protection from fuel fires.

Fire Blanket

The wool fire blanket fulfills two purposes. It is very effective for smothering fires, either on the boat or for wrapping around burning victims. Its other use is for hypothermia protection, and wool retains heat even when wet. Fire blankets come in watertight containers and should be mounted in an easily accessible place.

Personal Flotation Devices (PFDs)

Every patrol watercraft should carry an assortment of PFDs. The number on board should equal your boat's maximum capacity. You should also have several child size vests, as an adult size is too small for children. At least two vests must be readily available. Store jackets in a dry accessible area. An important point is that Type III or V jackets are the only ones comfortable enough to wear constantly. Jacket colors should be bright yellow or international orange color to facilitate locating the wearer. Commercial types have reflective material stitched on them. Let's quickly look at each type and note its uses and design:

TYPE I PFD: Designed to be used in rough water, these provide the best protection. The design is such to turn an unconscious victim face up, with the mouth well out of the water. You should have a minimum of two of these on your boat, one for yourself and the other for your partner. Also use these on cooperative handcuffed prisoners.

TYPE II PFD: This type is commonly known as a "horse collar," and you should carry two on the boat to use for prisoners who must be forcibly handcuffed. They are relatively inexpensive but may not turn a victim face up.

TYPE III PFD: These come in many shapes and styles, the most common being the vest type. Vests are designed mainly for comfort and may not provide enough buoyancy in rough water or even keep your face up. Other Type III rated PFDs are quite different and include the "float coat" and the "survival/exposure suit." These were discussed earlier and form an important component of your survival gear.

TYPE IV PFDS: Basically found in two types, the cushion and the ring buoy, these are not made to be worn but are only auxiliary equipment. We recommend the cushions for sitting and as emergency floats. Every boat, however, should have a Type IV ring buoy. Rigged with 25 feet of line, these can be thrown quite accurately, even under the arms of a person exhibiting the Instinctive Drowning Response. The line should be attached to a float at the bitter end to act as a stopper knot and to assist recovering the line in case it goes overboard. A better arrangement is to connect the ring buoy to a "throw bag." The ring buoy should be permanently mounted in a convenient location for rapid use.

TYPE V PFD: These are inflatable PFDs of new design, with inflatable compartments and buoyant material. Some are inflated by breath and others with CO_2 cartridge. Currently they have a "conditional" USCG rating. These may be the best type for watercraft patrol officers, as deflated they are more trim and comfortable than Type IIIs but when inflated give Type I protection. The "conditional" rating means they must be worn when the boat is underway or they don't count as a PFD. For a well-equipped patrol boat, this is not an issue.

Throw Bag

This device consists of a length of line stowed in a canvas/nylon bag. To use, hold the end of the line in the weak hand and throw the bag to the victim. The line feeds smoothly from the bag, avoiding the problem of line tangling. A throw bag coupled to a ring buoy is the best marriage of both devices.

First-Aid Kit System

Most commercial first-aid kits fail to meet the specific needs of watercraft and conservation officers. The Arizona Game and Fish Department unsuccessfully tried for many years to find a commercial first-aid kit that would meet the varied needs of its field officers.

In 1985, a group of officers, which included myself as Regional Supervisor, and two Wildlife Managers (Barrett Edgar and Mike Holloran) who were EMTs, made a recommendation to the Department regarding agency-supplied first-aid kits. We knew that our field officers encountered a variety of first-aid problems, from cut fingers, to serious traumas such as car accidents, gunshot wounds, and "prop chops." We also considered

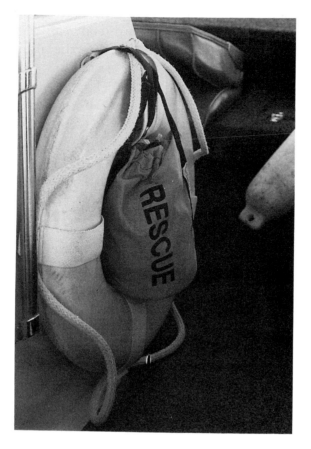

Figure 8. A centrally mounted ring buoy with a throwing line is an immediate lifesaver. Using a throw bag with the buoy will control the line storage problem.

that other departmental personnel had other needs for a first-aid kit. This made it impossible to design an agency-wide kit. At that time, the agency issue was a 16-unit "personal" kit, completely inadequate for anything but minor injuries, and automatically issued only to motor vehicles and watercraft.

Our recommendation was for the Department to adopt four different kits. These would not be separate kits but would build upon each other as the training and mission of the employee changed. The Department immediately accepted our recommendation, and the following describes this first-aid kit system.

First, we eliminated the 16-unit kits, replacing them with expanded "36-unit kits" for issue to every vehicle and watercraft. This is now our

Figure 9. The throw bag is a lightweight lifesaving device. It stows its line in a neat package that pays out as it is thrown.

standard first-aid kit, which has been expanded to include trauma items and still contain supplies for employee self-help.

The second level kit is known as the "first responder kit," issued to officers who complete a 16-hour "First Responder" course, and is renewed every two years. They carry this kit on both watercraft and land patrol assignments. This kit is primarily a trauma kit, as self-help items come from their "36-unit kit."

Field officers rated as EMTs are issued an additional "EMT kit." This kit, coupled with the 36-unit kit and the First Responder kit, provides EMTs with items appropriate for their expertise.

Patrol watercraft are equipped with the "watercraft kit" which remains in the patrol boats.

After four years of use, we re-evaluated the kits, removing some items adding others. This system has worked well and a similar system should work for you. Whatever kit you use, you should make sure that it meets your needs and is applicable to your patrol area. You may have to add extra items to bring it up to your standards.

Following is a list of items which make up the Arizona Game and Fish Department's first-aid kit system.

36-Unit First-Aid Kit

One 36-unit metal box, 16 1″ × 3″ plastic adhesive bandages, three 2″ gauze bandages, two 3″ offset compresses, six 4″ Telfa compresses, four 4″ gauze bandages, two triangular bandages, three 24″ × 72″ gauze bandages, one can Pyro-Cain burn spray, 12 Nox-A–Sting swabs, one tube medicated ointment, three 8″ × 8″ dressings, one roll 1″ adhesive tape, one instant ice pack, one instant heat pack, and one foil rescue blanket.

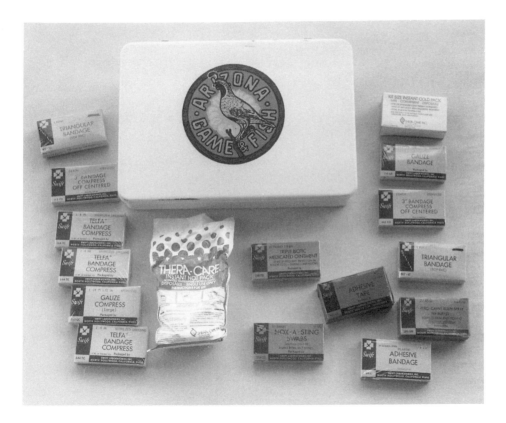

Figure 10. A 36-unit first-aid kit is standard issue in all watercraft and vehicles. This is a personal first-aid kit designed to take care of small everyday problems.

First Responder Kit

One 8″ × 18″ canvas bag, ten cleansing wipes, two triangular bandages, two oval eye pads, four 4″ × 15′ roller gauze, two 3″ × 15′ roller gauze, one pocket mask with one-way valve, one 4″ elastic bandage, two 8″ × 10″

Surgi-pads, four 10" × 30" multi-trauma dressings, ten Betadine packets, five tongue depressors, five assorted airways, three ¾" × 31" coated metal ladder splints, one large Dyna-Med cervical collar, one medium Dyna-Med cervical collar, one small Dyna-Med cervical collar, one 8" rescue shears, one foil rescue blanket, two 1" Dermicel tape, 16 1" plastic adhesive bandages, three knuckle bandages, one tube of instant glucose, one Sawyer Extractor snakebite kit, six pairs of surgical gloves, one bottle sterile water (250cc), two gunshot bandages, one D-cell strobe light and battery, one Wilderness signal kit, one 90-second Sky Marker smoke, one mini-light (or penlight) with batteries.

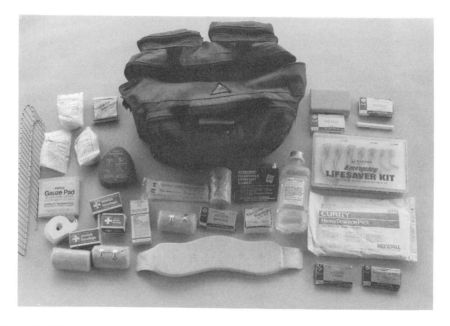

Figure 11. The "first responder" kit is issued to qualified officers and is designed to handle trauma emergencies.

EMT Kit

One activated charcoal poison antidote kit, one blood pressure kit, one stethoscope.

Watercraft Kit

One fire blanket and plastic box, one burn sheet, one bottle sterile water (250 cc), one long back board with straps, one oxygen bottle with

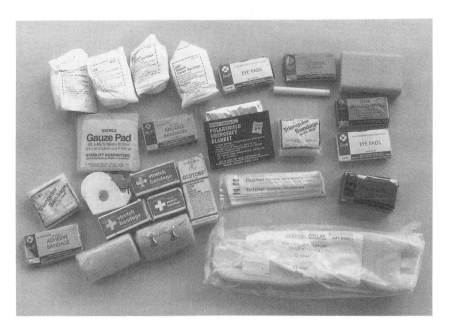

Figure 12. This displays more of the contents of the first responder kit. This kit, coupled with the 36-unit kit and the "watercraft" kit provides the officer with a wide variety of first-aid materials.

regulator and mask, one head and neck immobilizer (fits on back board).

Signaling Devices

We are very dependent upon our radio systems, but radio communication is impossible in many remote places in a watercraft officer's patrol area. Communication with other agencies, or responding emergency vehicles, may not be possible. Likewise, equipment failure may prevent radio communication. This is why you need to keep an inventory of signaling devices. Some are more effective than radio communication.

Signal Kit

A good kit of this type typically contains two or three hand-held aerial flares, a 60–90-second smoke grenade, a signal mirror and a whistle. These items fit in a plastic container small enough for a glove box or First Responder kit.

Signal Mirror

This small mirror is an underrated device, because it's the most valuable daytime signaling method you can have. Mirror flashes have been observed up to 100 miles from their source, under ideal conditions.[1] This makes the mirror an effective way to signal airplanes or a responding emergency helicopter on a bright sunlit day. The commercial mirrors have instructions printed on the back and a small aiming hole.

Smoke Grenades

These are available from commercial sources and are most effective on clear and calm days. Smoke signals have been observed from as far as 50 miles away.[2] To be visible, smoke must contrast with your background. High winds, snow, or rain disperse smoke and reduce its visibility. Some grenades are waterproof and will float while dispensing smoke. Besides showing your location to an aircraft, smoke will also show wind direction and approximate velocity.

Ground Flares

These produce light by chemical means. Highway flares are cheap but produce much less light than signaling flares and also produce a hot ash. Marine flares are designed to produce brilliant red or white light of about 500 candlepower and burn for about two minutes.[3]

Aerial Flares

These come in several forms and are designed for either day or night use. You should be familiar with each type, its limitations and its uses.

Hand-held rocket flares produce a bright fireball easily seen by aircraft. They are designed to be either low altitude or high altitude with corresponding burn times.

Pen gun flares are activated by a .45 caliber cartridge fired from a hand-held device and can reach an altitude of 400 to 500 feet.

Meteor flares are made for 12 gauge, 25mm and 37mm launchers, and burn at around 10,000 candlepower. Depending on weather, they can be seen by aircraft as far away at ten miles and by ships at 20 miles.[4]

Water Dye Marker

Also known as "sea marker," this is water-soluble dye powder. When dispersed under ideal conditions, this fluorescent light green dye is easily seen from an aircraft.

Signal Panel

The disposable foil emergency blanket may be used as a signaling device. The military uses a "paulin signal" panel. This is a 7 by 11 feet rubberized nylon panel with one yellow side and one blue side. By folding it in patterns and locating it for maximum visibility, messages can be sent to rescue aircraft.[5] The commercially available "space blanket," silver on one side and colored on the other, can serve the same purpose. This item may be helpful for marking a specific location for a helicopter. The military signaling panel code takes practice to learn, and few people would know what it means. For this reason it has limited uses.

Electronic Signals

Apart from normal radio communications, a "personal locator beacon" is set to transmit a distress code. Some are designed to be waterproof. A satellite monitoring system, known as "SARSAT," is in place to help locate persons in distress and transmit their location to rescue units. If using a beacon, you should leave it on until rescue arrives.

Whistle or Air Horn

Your voice is a poor way to call for help. Whistles or air horns project sound farther and conserve personal energy.

Law Enforcement Equipment

Patrol Boat Identification

Patrol boats must be marked with agency identity. Depending on your mission, however, there are three basic ways to mark a patrol watercraft.

High Visibility Enforcement Watercraft

High visibility markings are the traditional patrol markings. Large agency logos combined with official color markings, agency title in large letters, visible blue light, antennas and chrome siren, all present the patrol watercraft profile. This is a good marking system to advertise your presence on the water. It's not, however, an effective marking system if you're trying to apprehend deliberate violators. The "halo" effect lasts only as long as your boat is visible.

Figure 13. This sheriff's boat displays "high-visibility" enforcement markings. It's necessary to advertise law enforcement "presence" on the water.

Low Visibility Enforcement Watercraft

Small agency logos, non-standard colors, small agency titles, fold-down blue lights, and concealed siren, eliminate the traditional patrol watercraft profile. Emblems are visible from a short distance when approaching subjects. This type of marking allows the patrol officers to get closer to violators before being detected.

Unmarked Watercraft

Completely unmarked, these watercraft are used for special operations and to target specific violations, not for normal watercraft patrol.

Watercraft Equipment

These items are specific to the patrol watercraft.

Blue Light

This usually consists of a large strobe or flashing blue light used to hail subject boats or to identify emergency situations. Some are permanently displayed while others are mounted on fold-down mounts. The

Figure 14. This state game and fish boat is an example of a "low-visibility" profile. It allows officers to get closer before being detected, yet provides official identity.

Figure 15. Collapsible blue lights enhance the "low-visibility" profile.

Figure 16. Mounting the siren in the helm, and covering the aperture with a speaker grill, helps eliminate the traditional police profile for a "low-visibility" patrol boat.

fold-down variety is for low visibility watercraft, where the absence of a blue light helps break the patrol boat profile. At night, the blue strobe can dazzle both the operator and subjects. A canvas bag, with a clear plastic window, is a helpful accessory for night operations, shielding the operator from the light's glare.

Siren

This is typically a chrome bell mounted on the gunnel and serves for directional sound projection. If your purpose is low visibility, however, you should locate the siren out of sight. One technique is to mount a vehicle siren in the helm and cover the siren opening with a speaker grill.

Police Radio

This is so basic that not much needs to be said about it. If you can get the type that combines the PA and siren controls with it, you'll reduce console clutter. If your agency allows, it's preferable to program other police and emergency frequencies in it. Cross-communications with other agencies on the water increases both your efficiency and safety.

Figure 17. Where would we be without our blue lights and sirens? This light is mounted on a fold-down mount, with the speaker bell behind the gunnel.

PA (Public Address System)

This is necessary for hailing other boats and controlling suspects. If yours works through your police radio, it eliminates one microphone and helps relieve your work load under stress.

VHF Marine Radio

Used by many agencies, this 42-channel radio is also an accessory on many pleasure craft. This allows for inter-agency communication, as well as communication with other boats, and provides a common emergency frequency.

Multi-Agency Scanner

If you do not have the ability for inter-agency communications, this allows you to scan other frequencies for information and emergency APBs.

Figure 18. The blue light cover is important for night operation if you don't want to be dazzled by your own light(s).

Boarding Lights

Permanently mounted on the port and starboard side of your console or gunnels, these high-intensity quartz-halogen lights provide intense illumination for night boarding operations. They should be mounted away from your location, so if they draw fire you won't be behind them. Mounted on your boat and controlled with independently mounted switches, they free your hands for providing cover or other boarding actions. Hand-held lights allow for specific light direction, because you can direct them where you need the most light, but they have one drawback: they take up one hand and divert your attention. If you are the cover officer, you won't be able to use your long gun effectively. It also shows your position to suspects, unless you make a habit of holding it well away from you with your weak hand.

Depth Sounder

This is a small, relatively inexpensive sonar unit used to locate fish and determine depth. When equipped with a moving paper and tracking pen, this is also known as a "chart recorder." Some watercraft officers can use these skillfully enough to locate bodies or submerged illegal nets.

Direction Finding Equipment

These devices range from simple helm-mounted compasses through sophisticated radar units and satellite navigation devices. You should know the types available in your area and become proficient in their use.

Video Camera

Some agencies which perform a high number of boardings, especially where the potential for narcotics seizures is high, have installed video cameras on their boats to record boardings. Mounted to cover the boarding area, these have served well in prosecutions. If you have access to one of the new portable types, you will find it quite handy in recording boating violations, such as careless operation, and record O.U.I. sobriety checks for later courtroom use. Video cameras are also helpful for making recordings for boating safety classes.

Trolling Motor

If you perform a lot of boating safety or fishermen checks, a heavy-duty trolling motor mounted on your bow can be very helpful. The foot pedal control leaves your hands free. The trolling motor also saves wear and tear on your engine as you move from one contact to another. Once you become skillful in its use, the motor provides a high degree of control during a boarding. I've installed two of these on boats in high-use areas, and officers who use them have given me very positive feedback on their practicality. Each motor should have its own deep-cycle battery. The plug-in allows overnight charging, using a vehicle battery charger from an external electrical source.

Baton Holder

If you use the straight or side-handle baton instead of the collapsible type that fits on your belt, you need a way to store it where you can reach it quickly. A couple of broomstick clamps attached to a convenient location in your watercraft serve to stow your baton.

Riot Gun and Rifle Holder

You must provide locking storage for these firearms. Electric gun locks are very secure, but an electrical failure will prevent the removal of the long gun. Unless in a cabin, they also expose the long guns to moisture. A locking dry storage compartment with a rubber-coated gun rack is a better method of storage. You should leave the compartment unlocked while on patrol, but if you are involved in emergency operations where you will be taking victims on board, or must leave the boat unattended, you must lock it. If the compartment is large enough, it can provide stowage for your gun belt when you have to remove and stow it.

Figure 19. A riot gun is essential. This one is mounted in a high, dry and out-of-the-way position inside a locking compartment.

Parachute Flares

These are available at most police supply stores. A cardboard tube is both the container and launcher for the flare. Upon firing, it projects a parachute flare hundreds of feet into the air and provides bright illumination for several minutes. An effective tactical tool, it may provide you with an edge during a night operation. It certainly will provide you with psychological superiority, as most suspects will be totally surprised and dazzled if they look at it. When seeking a suspect hiding from you or trying to apprehend someone operating without lights, these flares will quickly provide the illumination you need.

Charts

You need a current and accurate set of charts for your patrol area. You should also have a set of topographical maps for the surrounding area in case you need to go ashore. Stow all maps in a dry location. Some map companies provide plastic laminated charts or have them printed on water-resistant paper.

Towing Harness

Described in Chapter 17, this device should be standard equipment on all patrol watercraft.

Maintenance Supplies

Properly maintained equipment is less likely to fail under use and stress. As a watercraft patrol officer, you're obliged to ensure that your equipment receives all necessary maintenance. You can perform certain minor tasks yourself, such as tightening nuts and bolts, changing props, and greasing hubs. Other work is better done in the shop and it's your responsibility to schedule it when necessary. Watercraft cleanliness is also important, because it's a conspicuous display of your proficiency. It also reduces maintenance problems. Besides tools necessary to do mechanical maintenance, you should also keep some small "housekeeping" items on board.

A pail can substitute for a bailer if necessary, but it also serves for soapy water for deck scrubbing and general cleaning.

Sponges are needed for washing your helm, seats, and general cleaning around the boat.

Glass wax is necessary with a fiberglass boat. The gelcoat needs a covering of wax, which, when applied, makes it easier to clean your hull of water scum and other unsightly deposits. Also, a good grade of vehicle wax applied to your engine will ease removal of grime and water spots.

Most boats have plastic windshields, making a can of plastic window cleaner necessary. Using other cleaners will cause a scratched and cloudy windshield.

You should also carry a couple cans of Marine Tex in order to cover the nicks in the gelcoat or fiberglass on your hull. The force of the water along your hull will cause the layers of fiberglass to separate if the hull is damaged through the gelcoat. Prompt repair of the hull with Marine

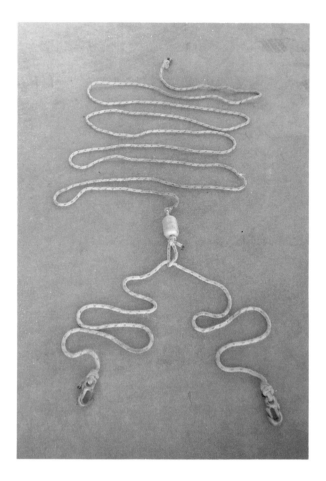

Figure 20. This is a towing harness with a bridle. Two hooks on the bridle attach to the patrol boat's transom, and the tow line's loop allows it to slide along the bridle. This gives a steady pull behind your boat while towing and makes it easier to control your steering.

Tex reduces drag and protects the fiberglass. Performing this needed maintenance on a frequent and timely basis should help reduce the need for costly hull repairs. Marine Tex can also be used to strengthen or "armor" portions of the hull that receive the most wear. When using, avoid getting any in your eyes. You should wear old clothes or coveralls, as it will not come out of clothing.

Personal Items

Some items are for your comfort, as well as your safety. An ice chest to store food and soft drinks is helpful, and some boats now have built-in insulated chests. Another personal necessity is some type of dry stowage for first-aid kits, ammunition, and citations. Sometimes an ice chest serves to store personal items to be kept dry, if another is available for food and drinks. When rigging a boat, remember to consider dry storage as an important item.

NOTES

1. *U.S. Air Force Survival Manual,* p. 464.
2. Ibid., p. 461.
3. *Sea Survival: The Boatman's Emergency Manual.* Farley and Huff, 1989, Page 33.
4. Ibid., p. 33.
5. *U.S. Air Force Survival Manual,* p. 462.

Chapter 22

THE IDEAL PATROL WATERCRAFT

Attempting to define an ideal watercraft is like trying to select the ideal hunting rifle for all types of game or one vehicle for multiple uses. A particular watercraft must be suitable to the water and the mission. Some administrators cause their own problems when they attempt to simplify purchasing procedures by selecting one model of "patrol boat" for universal use. Unfortunately, their attempts usually result in a boat being "no good nowhere." In this section, we'll discuss some attributes we feel an ideal patrol boat should have. It won't be 100 percent perfect and won't please everyone, but from our experience these features apply to a law enforcement watercraft.

The boat should be of open construction in order to allow officers to move around the boat unimpeded. You should not have to climb on your knees to reach the bow, nor wiggle through a narrow windshield. You need room to handcuff a resisting subject and a deck large enough to transport a victim strapped to a back board. You should be able to stand up comfortably under the shade/weather cover. You should also be able to stand up at the helm, and the windshield should be high enough to protect your face from debris or insects.

Your boat should be proportioned to the boats you are trying to regulate. You shouldn't have to reach over your head to grab the rails of a boat you are trying to inspect, nor should you have to lean over the gunnels to inspect another boat.

It should be compatible with the assigned waters, which means that it should keep you afloat and dry. If bad weather and rough water are the rule, you should have a boat large enough to handle the seas and an enclosed cabin to keep you warm and dry.

Your boat should be fast enough to catch a violator within a reasonable distance. It should come up onto plane quickly in order to ensure safe forward vision. It should be of quality construction and the engine should be reliable. It should be large enough to provide stowage for all your gear, and it should be stable so that you and your partner don't have to worry about capsizing while handling a resisting suspect.

It should offer you cover and concealment from gunfire, if possible. Some companies offer armored helms, for example. If you work in a high threat level area, look into one of these. You should be allowed to add items necessary for the successful completion of your mission.

The ideal boat will be easy to clean and maintain. It should look sharp.

This may appear to be preaching, and maybe it is, but management has a moral obligation to provide you with the best equipment and training possible to help you carry out your job safely. Management owes you honest leadership and support. You should feel proud of your boat, your department, your job and yourself.

An efficient and sturdy craft will help do all of the above and more, if it matches your needs and the water and mission you are assigned.

PART IV. WATERCRAFT OFFICER TRAINING

Chapter 23

DEVELOPING A TRAINING PROGRAM

Every agency with watercraft patrol officers must invest in active training for them. If your agency has few watercraft officers, it may be more cost-effective to attend a training program conducted by a larger department. Regardless of agency size, you may wish to provide your own training or provide the same opportunities to sister agencies.

In this chapter, we'll discuss the establishment of a watercraft officer training program. You may use this technique for a large inter-agency training program or for designing one or two specialized or advanced courses. For the purposes of our discussion, we'll assume that your need is an extensive watercraft training program. You can use segments of this for less complex projects.

Step 1: Needs Assessment

The first phase in program development is the "Needs Assessment" before you consider the types of courses you wish to present. You must not skip this stage, because careful research and preparation here will save you considerable time and resources later. It will also ensure that the training you offer is relevant to your agency's role and work load. To complete the needs assessment, you must answer the following questions:

1. What does your enabling law dictate as your task? Are you required to perform certain jobs, i.e. maintenance of navigational aids, search and rescue operations, boating education, noise enforcement, etc.?

2. What are your agency's mission and objectives?

3. What are your community needs and expectations? What does the public think you should be doing? Do they depend on you for assistance? If so, what kind?

4. What are your internal organizational needs? Do you have citizen advisory boards or commissions which you must solicit for input? Do you have an accurate idea of what upper management expects? Are there special liabilities? If you have an open assignment, you need to ask your upper management about the limits of the program. This will reveal

whether you really have an open assignment or if there are any "hidden agendas" you need to identify. If there are any such, the earlier you know, the easier it will be to work with them. This is also the time to consider any historical problems you may have encountered. What has happened in the patrol areas that indicate training or retraining?

5. You need to consider your budget. What economic resources can you use? Do you have any strategies for obtaining supporting funds?

6. What do your officers need and expect from your training program? What is the current level of their training and what else do they want? You must ask them and consider their answers.

7. You must also contact other agencies to solicit cooperation, such as sharing of resources. If you have good rapport with their officers, they may even be willing to share their mistakes with you, which can be more valuable than tangible resources.

In the February/March 1990 issue of *Small Craft Advisory* (NASBLA Vol. V, No. 3), all fifty states presented a set of basic courses and training requirements for their watercraft officers. For your convenience, we have sorted this extensive list by topic, plus added a few of our own.

ENVIRONMENTAL SURVIVAL SKILLS: Cold water, rough water and rapids, creeks, rabies and Lyme disease, low water dams, hypothermia, river paddling skills, weather, and heat emergencies.

FIREARM SKILLS: Basic skills in sidearms, shotguns and rifles.

FIRST-AID SKILLS: AIDS, First Responder, CPR.

LAWS: Environmental, legal updates, customs, pollution, marine toilet, hazardous materials, endangered species, commercial fisheries, noise regulations, Indian artifacts, game regulations, fish regulations, juvenile laws, charter boat regulations, navigational aids, mooring management, liquor law violations, drug violations.

ENFORCEMENT TECHNIQUES: Handcuffing, speed-cuffing, defensive tactics, straight baton, side-handle baton, collapsible baton, chemical weapons, verbal diffusion, pressure point management, joint manipulation, human relations, interpersonal communication, photography, VCRs, domestic violence, vehicle assaults, verbal judo, active countermeasures, sexual harassment, deadly force, escalation-of-force continuum, electronic surveillance, sonar search, forensics, flashlight defense, firearms retention and take-aways, felony stops, low and high risk boardings, inspections, search and seizure, tactical communications, stolen boats, accident investigations.

NAVIGATION SKILLS: Piloting, radar and LORAN, night navigation, charting.

OPERATION SKILLS: Inboard, outboard, and jet operation, engine maintenance and troubleshooting, trailering, basic seamanship.

O.U.I. ENFORCEMENT: Field sobriety tests, determining O.U.I. operators.

PHYSICAL SKILLS: Swimming, annual physical testing, physical fitness, health maintenance.

RESCUE TECHNIQUES: Fast-water rescue, heavy-duty rescue, towing and rescue, river rescue, ice rescue, victim extraction, fire fighting, rescue boat handling.

SPECIALITY SKILLS: UL/USCG Accident Investigation Course, USCG Boarding Officer School, USCG Boating Skills and Seamanship Course, horizontal gaze nystagmus school, Intoxilizer school, Scuba school, emergency medical technician program, paramedic program, drug recognition and interdiction school, field training officer, Swift Water Rescue Course, FMP Marine Law Enforcement Skills, Tactics and Investigations Course, AZGFD Watercraft Law Enforcement and Survival Tactics Course, basic police rifle school, advanced firearms school.

Step 2: Identification of Courses

After you have answered the questions above and have a feeling for what you need, the next step is straightforward. Based upon what you discovered from the "needs assessment," make a list of information, knowledge, and skills you wish to present.

Sort this list by groups and rank them according to priority. You should also consider that some training is relatively simple and its presentation will be inexpensive. Other training will be complex and may require complicated logistics and training facilities. Generally, schools whose objectives relate to motor coordination skills require more manpower expense than the information transmittal courses.

For simplicity and logical grouping arrangement, you should consider that police training comes in three categories:

Basic training: All peace officers in the United States attend the "Academy." The curriculum varies but centers around basic police skills. Check with your academy and find out what skills your people learn. Many agencies conduct a "post-academy" school. Scrutinize the topics in this school.

Specialty schools: Listed above in Step 1, these schools and courses cover special topics and usually require complex logistics. Such schools typically last from three days to two weeks or longer.

Advanced Techniques: These classes provide officers with the opportunity to broaden their basic or specialty training skills. Advanced techniques may also focus on "team" training.

Step 3: Development of Instructor Cadre

Once you've decided what you want to have taught, you need to select the teachers. The development of an instructor cadre may be the most critical stage of a successful program, because poor instructors can ruin the best school.

You may not have the internal resources to conduct all of your training requirements. Selecting outside instructors or schools requires careful consideration regarding course material and objectives. Obviously, you'll use only outside resources that fill your needs, and provide training you can't provide with agency resources. For the most part, however, you'll use in-house instructors.

Selecting and developing an in-house instructor cadre is critical to the success of your program. You'll need instructors with experience and skill in the subjects they teach. They must also have a positive attitude and have a desire to teach fellow employees and help their students and their agency. They should be volunteers. Instructors who are lazy, or have bad attitudes, have no place in any training program. Training has long-term effects on an agency, and the wise leader knows that training is a key factor in motivational development.

After selecting instructors, you must provide training to enhance their ability to instruct. For instance, they may need instruction in preparing lesson plans and conducting a block of instruction or developing a slide program.

After their teaching instruction is completed, your agency should present formal letters of appointment, certificates, and some type of insignia to wear on their uniforms. Also, some agencies have found ways to provide supplemental income for instructors, covering the time they are assigned to training. This is a good way to motivate your instructors, as recognition is the best reward for a job well done.

You also must assign your instructors to their various training assignments through a formal process. You must designate chief instructors and assistants, as well as their specific tasks. Generally, chief instructors are responsible for coordinating and overseeing logistics and assistant instructors.

Figure 1. Development of a competent instructor cadre is a vital component of successful long-term training. In this instructor training class, one of the authors, Turner, is explaining the safety procedures for the watercraft tactical course to a class of watercraft instructors.

Step 4. Development of Lesson Plans

Once your needs assessment, course identification, and instructor cadre appointments are completed, your next task is to develop your courses. Training imparts the fundamentals of knowledge, awareness, and hands-on skills, and ends with testing and qualification. All courses should address each of these fundamentals.

The lesson plan is the backbone of a training course. This is why you must spend the time to lay each lesson plan out carefully. You may have these developed externally or internally. External development will rely on consultants or personnel from other agencies. If you decide to proceed with external lesson plan development, make sure that the writers receive specific instructions on your desires. Reserve the right to approve course objectives before granting authority to proceed.

Internal development of lesson plans should fall on the shoulders of your instructor cadre, because you've selected them for their skill and experience. Now is the time to tap their knowledge. Prepare an outline to show lesson plan format. Some agencies use official forms for lesson plans.

Course size should be planned for a maximum number of students. Generally, the more students you have, the longer it takes to cover your material. Optimal class size appears to be about twenty students. Larger classes require many additional resources, and significantly smaller classes aren't cost-effective. Another reason is that it's easier to set up schedules and order supplies for a fixed maximum number of students.

A lesson plan should state: Course Title, Course ID Number, Course Goal, Training Objectives (what the students should be able to accomplish), Instructor References, Logistics (training aids, facilities, materials, other assistance needed, etc.), Safety Considerations, Method of Presentation (lecture, demonstration, hands-on, etc.), Level of Instruction (basic, speciality, advanced), a comprehensive Course Outline, a Written Final Exam, a Qualification Exercise (if appropriate), and a Student Course Evaluation.

Remember the training adage "tell them what you're going to tell them, tell them, tell them what you told them," when you're preparing your lesson plans. It pays to be redundant.

Step 5. Course Presentation

The way an instructor presents a course reflects upon his competence and it makes the difference between meaningful training and a waste of time. Design your courses with a suitable number of breaks. Generally, a ten-minute break for every fifty minutes of instruction is best.

There are many ways to present course material, but a course which varies its methods is usually more effective in promoting retention of subject material. A classroom lecture is efficient in passing on knowledge to a large number of students. A "multi-media" presentation is more effective because it combines lecture with slide presentations, movies, and training videos. Practical exercises, where appropriate, fortify the material being presented and help develop motor skills.

Step 6. Course Testing and Qualification

Testing is a major component of a course, providing a "pass/fail" mechanism to weed out substandard performers. A written test will help you objectively document deficiencies. If the course objective requires certain motor skills, a qualification test will be necessary.

Step 7. Course Evaluation

Finally, you need feedback to suggest ways of improving your course. A good way to obtain feedback is to ask the students. Their anonymous course evaluations will help you correct deficiencies and may even help you expand the course. If you're an administrator, course evaluations will assist in monitoring the abilities of your instructors.

Step 8. Course Certification

Successful students need to be rewarded for their efforts. A well-designed and formally presented certificate provides tangible evidence of their efforts. You should also send a copy of their course records to their supervisor for inclusion in their agency personnel record.

If your course meets criteria established by certifying organizations, obtain certification. Recognition from outside groups adds prestige to your courses and also helps if your agency is challenged as to its training. State Law Enforcement Advisory Boards, the National Rifle Association, and other groups provide certification. Look for some in your local area, find out their standards, and see if you can accommodate them in your course.

Step 9. Course Logistics

The ability to determine logistical requirements, anticipate problems, and provide for solutions in advance is an attribute possessed by few people. Often, a high quality course, taught by a capable instructor, will fail because of an inability to handle the logistics.

Getting the right personnel, materials, and equipment to the right place, at the right time, and in an operable condition to be used for a class is the objective of good logistics preparation. If you've ever sat for 30 minutes in a course waiting for the instructor to find a projector bulb, you can understand what's at stake. Do your best to avoid similar embarrassing situations.

I find that a mental exercise of "visualization" before a course is presented gives me a good idea of what will go wrong. I go through each phase of the course and list what I need, what problems might occur (always consider safety issues), and what might fail.

As part of this process, I have developed a Logistical Work Sheet. This work sheet simplifies logistical planning. Course area, title, chief instructor and secondary instructors are identified, as well as instructor materials, student materials, course materials, and safety considerations needed for the successful completion of the training. Limiting class size to a maximum of twenty students also helps with the planning efforts.

If you depend on others to provide some of your logistics, you must ensure that they meet their obligations. If you assume that someone else is going to do what they promised, then you should be prepared to assume the embarrassment and the responsibility if they fail. Make sure what you need is available, where you need it, and at the time you need it.

Give others a break, and don't wait until the last minute to place your supply orders or other logistical requests. Some complex courses may need more than six months' lead time.

Step 10. Course Facilities

Select a training location that provides a comfortable environment for your students. It should have all the resources necessary for completion of your course. It should also be located near sleeping, eating and off-duty recreation facilities.

Step 11. Course Advertisement and Scheduling

The earlier you can schedule your course, the better. Prospective students and assistant instructors need as much lead time as possible. You should try to have a full class, even if you have to invite personnel from other agencies to participate. Early scheduling also allows for advertisement of the course, thus resulting in greater participation.

Step 12. Teach the Class and Keep Records

Finally, you can conduct the class. To avoid personal liability, make it your habit to not deviate from the lesson plan.

Don't tell "war stories," unless they serve to fortify the point you just made. Make sure these stories are part of the lesson plan. Never project your personal bias or make "off-the-record" comments. You should never take advantage of a "captive audience" by using it as a forum for telling jokes. Humorous antidotes are valuable speaking tools, but they must relate to the subject. Always avoid ethnic and sexual topics. Not only do these remarks spoil your professional image, but they may come back to haunt you.

If one of your students gets into trouble, the first thing he'll use in his defense is "he told me to do it that way during his training course." Or, "I failed the class because of prejudice, as he told several jokes which showed his bias against me." If you can't prove you didn't, you are going to suffer.

The best advice to avoid liability problems is to "go by the book" and keep records. Always make sure your comments relate to the lesson plan. If you do so, testimony to a court or board of inquiry will be easy.

You should keep a personal instructor's record file, with records for every class you've taught. In this file should be a copy of the lesson plan for each course. If your training program is dynamic, as it should be, you will be updating your lesson plans continually. This is why your file should have the specific lesson plan you used for each course.

Your file should also contain copies of handouts used, an agenda, copies of written exams, records of performance, safety instructions (always have these in writing, you may even want to have the student sign a list stating that they have received the safety handout, and understand its contents), and a student attendance sheet.

Make it a habit to "CYA," because following the above advice will pay off in the future. Officer survival does not just apply to street survival. A training officer must always consider his areas of potential liability and make efforts, in advance, to protect himself.

Chapter 24

A RECOMMENDED WATERCRAFT OFFICER TRAINING PROGRAM

As mentioned earlier, training can be categorized into basic, specialty and advanced training. Our watercraft training program will fall into the specialty and advanced training categories.

Prospective students must have completed basic training, including academy and post-training. They must know how to swim and have some familiarity with watercraft. Having passed the academy and post-academy courses, they'll have basic proficiency with the handgun, shotgun, and other police-related skills, which are prerequisites for the watercraft course.

Watercraft patrol officer training is a specialized topic and the traditional "boot camp" atmosphere doesn't fit. The purpose of the course is to teach a variety of related topics and to produce successful graduates, not wash out prospective officers. A failure means wasting very expensive training, which emphasizes the point that only suitable candidates should be in the class. A high rate of washouts alerts you to a problem with the lesson plan, the instructor, or the logistics.

It's important to let students know at the outset that the course will be hard work, not play, to forestall the impression that there will be much free time to "party." Close coordination is essential, to use each hour of the training day effectively, and avoid unproductive gaps between classes. Another way to induce students to devote time to the course is to provide handouts pertaining to the following day's material. Instructors should encourage students to study the printed material in the evenings, to get a start on the next day's work.

We feel strongly that at the end of the training day, students should be tired from having put in a full and productive day. However, extreme fatigue is mind-numbing and detrimental to learning, which is why there should be a ten-minute break at the end of each hour of instruction, where possible. On land, this is usually workable because instructors can have a class recess at fifty-minute intervals. On the water, students will have to rest when they can. Boat handling and firearms stages are typically all-day sessions and can easily take ten or twelve hours. Students should bring insulated containers of cold or hot drinks, box lunches, and a few creature comforts.

Figure 1. During field training exercises, students and instructors must take breaks when they can. Here, several instructors eat lunch on a pontoon boat while waiting for their next group of students.

Time spent on the water is tiring, and instructors must monitor students carefully to ensure that they don't exhaust them. Instructors should be prepared to provide sunblock, safety glasses, ear protectors and water for students who have forgotten theirs.

"Practice does not make perfect: only perfect practice makes perfect." This wisdom comes from Bruce Siddle, noted law enforcement trainer, who knows whereof he speaks. Competent instructors know this and watch their students to make sure they do not reinforce bad habits.

If an instructor allows his students to practice the wrong habits, they'll probably react that way in a real-life situation. A well-known example is allowing revolver shooters to put their empty cases in a hand or pocket. Another bad habit, very relevant to watercraft survival, is allowing officers to practice reloading without taking cover behind the gunnel. If a semi-auto shooter has his head and shoulders above the gunnel when he drops his magazine, he may drop it into the water! We've seen a student lose his magazine this way. In a real-life armed encounter, he may lose his life by forgetting to use available cover.

Watercraft officer instruction is expensive because of the equipment involved and because training is intensive, requiring hands-on instruction. Classroom sessions usually are team taught but have a high student-to-instructor ratio. On water exercises, the ratio of instructors to students will be 1:2.

Following is a recommended speciality training program for watercraft officers:

WATERCRAFT OFFICER TRAINING PROGRAM,
Course Outline

Day One
>   Introduction
>   Communications
>   Watercraft Laws and Regulations
>   Enforcement Procedures
>   Patrol Procedures

Day Two
>   Stolen Watercraft Investigations
>   Watercraft Accident Investigations

Day Three
>   Operation Under the Influence
>   Patrol Watercraft Rigging
>   Patrol Watercraft Maintenance

Day Four
>   Navigational Aids
>   Line Handling
>   Written Exam
>   Water Safety Skills

Day Five
>   Watercraft Operation

Day Six
>   Watercraft Tactical Techniques

Day Seven
>   Watercraft Firearms

Now let's take a look at the specifics of the program, which includes the course name, length, description, safety considerations, other considerations, and logistical notations. Many of these courses can be taught separately. Please note that "Safety Considerations" refer to the safety needs the instructor must consider while conducting the course.

DAY ONE

Title: INTRODUCTION
Length: 30 minutes
Objectives:

Students will be able to explain the schedule for the training course, course overview, course development and need, and their personal needs and expectations for off-duty and on-duty activities. They'll also be able to describe the safety rules which govern the course.

Description:

A lecture which provides the students with an overview of the 56-hour course, handouts, course materials, student supply needs, schedule for the 7 days, breaks, local accommodations, and other items about the course which will let the student know what is to come, both on duty and after hours.

Safety Considerations:

This is to advise students of the hazards involved with hands-on training. They will become aware of the safety rules for various aspects of the school, such as the need for sunblock, ear and eye protection, PFD needs, safety areas, ammo and firearm control, and swimming requirements. The instructor should determine what safety supplies he needs to furnish.

Other Considerations:

Sack lunches, personal water or soft drinks, and other personal comfort items should be discussed.

Special Logistics:

Course material handouts, sign up sheet, introduction of instructors and students, class roster, course agenda.

Title: COMMUNICATIONS
Length: 30 minutes
Objectives:

Students will be able to explain communication procedures for emergency messages during the course. Students will be able to explain agency communication procedures, and on-water radio procedures.

Description:

This lecture will familiarize the student with the procedures for accepting and transmitting emergency messages while attending class. This includes location of phones and other communication equipment. The instructor will review agency policies and procedures for using the radio net or other communication facilities while on watercraft patrol.

Safety Considerations:

Location of emergency facilities.

Title: WATERCRAFT LAWS AND REGULATIONS
Length: Four hours
Objectives:

Students will be able to detect violations of boating laws and regulations, and be able to identify the appropriate statutes.

Figure 2. An instructor uses the lecture format while discussing the details of the state watercraft laws.

Description:

This lecture class covers all laws, rules and regulations that pertain to the students' patrol duties. The instructors explain the various laws, as well as ways to detect specific types of violations.

Other Considerations:

Appropriate handouts, slide show and video presentations, as well as demonstration objects. This subject is ideal for team-teaching.

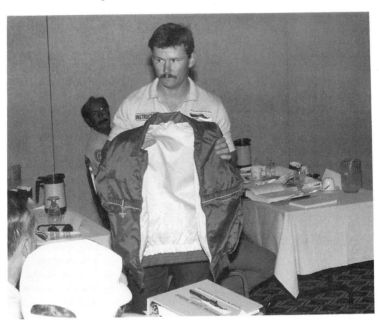

Figure 3. Handouts and other visual materials greatly enhance a lecture. A Type IV float coat is the subject of this demonstration.

Title: ENFORCEMENT PROCEDURES

Length: One hour and 30 minutes

Objectives:

Students will be able to explain agency policies and procedures in regards to the enforcement of boating laws. Students will be able to issue citations and make arrests following agency policies.

Description:

In a lecture setting, students learn the agency philosophy of boating enforcement. Instructors cover policies and procedures for issuing citations and making physical arrests.

Other Considerations:

Multi-media presentation. Note that using slides, videotapes, etc., help keep the subject matter vivid.

Title: PATROL PROCEDURES
Length: One hour and 30 minutes
Objectives:

Students will be able to explain agency procedures for patrol assignments, as well as types of patrols and patrol objectives.

Figure 4. A student and instructor go over the fine points of calibrating a sound meter used in noise enforcement.

Description:

In a classroom environment, students will learn agency procedures for patrol activities. Instructors will describe various types of patrols, as well as agency objectives for various patrol efforts. Coordination with other agencies will be discussed.

Other Considerations:

Multi-media presentation.

DAY TWO

Title: STOLEN WATERCRAFT INVESTIGATIONS
Length: Four hours
Objectives:

Students will be able to explain the Hull Identification Number (HIN) system and be able to detect altered or false HINs. They will be able to conduct a stolen watercraft investigation and to seize and impound suspected stolen boats following agency procedures.

Description:

A lecture will introduce students to HINs and the varied techniques suspects use to alter them. Other topics include stolen boat operations, as well as inspections of stolen boats. This will include techniques for the identification of potential stolen boats, hidden HINs, registration alterations, and accessory equipment identification. Students will learn the proper agency procedures for seizure, impoundment and forfeiture of stolen boats, including investigative techniques. Reports, NCIC files and other available resources will be discussed.

Other Considerations:

Multi-media and team teaching.

Special Logistics:

Forfeited boat with altered HIN.

Title: WATERCRAFT ACCIDENT INVESTIGATIONS
Length: Four hours
Objectives:

Students will be able to investigate watercraft accidents and complete all agency investigative forms. They will be able to determine causes of different types of accidents and will be able to record accurate data from the accident scene.

Description:

This subject is a lecture, supplemented by visual aids. Students will cover agency responsibilities and procedures for accident investigations, as well as proper reporting of investigative results. The collection of evidence as well as techniques for determining causes of accidents will be covered. Students will be separated into work groups and provided with a sample accident for study, including photographs and paperwork. They will collaborate to determine the cause.

Other Considerations:
    Multi-media and team teaching.
Special Logistics:
    Sample accident package.

DAY THREE

Title: OPERATION UNDER THE INFLUENCE
Length: Six hours
Objectives:
    Students will be able to detect and apprehend suspects operating
under the influence of alcohol. Students will be able to evaluate extent

Figure 5. The class on "O.U.I." enforcement covers lecture material.

of O.U.I. involvement and be able to utilize proper field sobriety
techniques. Students will be able to complete a successful investigation,
prepare written reports, and develop a successful prosecution.
Description:
    This presentation is a combination of lecture and hands-on activities.
Students will view current statistics and studies detailing the problem
with O.U.I. operators. They will receive instruction on the effects of

alcohol and drugs on a person's mental and physical state. They will be exposed to various techniques for identifying boats operated by intoxicated subjects. Students will perform field sobriety (impairment) tests. They will have available an intoxicated volunteer on which the instructors will demonstrate proper field interview procedures. Instructors will coach the students on proper procedures for completing a field O.U.I. investigation and paperwork, including pitfalls and techniques for a successful prosecution.

Other Considerations:

This should be a multi-media presentation.

Special Logistics:

An intoxicated volunteer is necessary. Equipment needed includes

Figure 6. The use of audiovisual materials, overhead projections and handouts makes this O.U.I. lecture a more powerful learning experience.

portable breath alcohol meters and an Intoxilizer, as well as O.U.I. forms. If possible, instructors should present profiles of intoxicated boaters. Printed matter includes handouts covering the effects of various substances on the human body.

Title: PATROL WATERCRAFT RIGGING
Length: One hour
Objectives:

Students will be able to properly prepare watercraft for patrol assignments. They will be familiar with safety equipment, lines, and on-board storage of equipment.

Description:

This lecture course focuses on the proper rigging of patrol watercraft. This includes attachment of lines and fenders, preparation of anchor lines, and the storage of PFDs, fire extinguishers, first-aid equipment and other rescue gear. Students will learn the optimum way to rig a patrol craft, according to applicable agency policies and procedures.

Other Considerations:

A slide show is the most effective way to teach this subject.

Title: PATROL WATERCRAFT MAINTENANCE
Length: One hour
Objectives:

Students will be able to explain the proper (short term, long term, and storage) maintenance procedures for patrol watercraft, engines, and trailers.

Description:

A lecture will cover the procedures necessary to maintain a patrol watercraft, trailer, and engine. Officer-applied maintenance as well as scheduled maintenance checks, troubleshooting, engine servicing, and trailer maintenance and repair will be covered. Instructors will explain how to prepare a watercraft for storage, as well as retrieval.

DAY FOUR

Title: NAVIGATIONAL AIDS
Length: One hour
Objectives:

Students will be able to describe the navigational aids in their patrol area. They will be able to explain their agency's responsibility for navigational aids if appropriate.

Description:

A lecture will cover the navigational aids and waterway marking system used in the agency area. Policies and procedures relating to the agency's responsibility for the navigational aid system will also be covered.

Other Considerations:

A slide show is an effective method to present the material for this class.

Title: LINE HANDLING

Length: One hour

Objectives:

Students will be able to tie basic marine knots and describe their proper use. Students will be able to explain proper line selection, storage, and use, especially in rescue operations.

Description:

This lecture is a refresher in basic marlinspike seamanship skills, designed to cover lines and their proper storage and use. Emphasis is on the use of lines in emergency situations and in daily activities. Students will have hands-on experience with tying the bowline, clove hitch, two half-hitches, sheet bend, square knot, anchor bend, and figure eight knot. They will learn how to belay a cleat, and wrap the end of a line, and the use of various types of line, such as hemp, polypropylene, nylon, etc., as well as each type's advantages and disadvantages for watercraft patrol work.

Special Considerations:

Overheads or handouts showing the steps in tying various knots.

Special Logistics:

One 3-foot length of ¼- or ⅜-inch line per student. Also required is an item around which to tie knots, i.e. pipe, chair leg, etc.

Title: WRITTEN EXAM

Length: One hour

Objective:

To determine if students have achieved the course objectives.

Description:

This should be a multiple-choice and "true/false" test covering the major subject material presented up to this point. One hundred questions are sufficient. Knowing that a test is forthcoming provides incentive for students to pay attention to the lecture and read the handouts.

Special Considerations:

Students score each other's test papers in class, and the instructor collects them when finished. An explanation of the correct answer should be given when the test is being corrected.

Special Logistics:

Appropriate number of blank tests.

Title: WATER SAFETY SKILLS
Length: Five hours
Objectives:

To familiarize officers with various water rescue techniques, associated hazards and personal survival. To introduce officers to in-water situations regarding uniforms, weights and PFDs. To familiarize officers with water entries, strokes, water exits, and in-water first-aid extraction techniques using the long back board.

Description:

A lecture and practical exercises presented to familiarize watercraft officers with basic water safety survival skills. The course outline and discussion are taken from the Arizona Game and Fish Department Lesson Plan; "Water Safety," by Don Turner, June 14, 1988.

Stage 1: Water Safety Lecture (two-hour presentation)

Personal Survival in the Water: This section covers the officer's survival in a water environment. The need for swimming skills is emphasized. Officers learn the problems with cramps, drown-proofing techniques and hypothermia; symptoms, causes, prevention, and treatment. Swift water problems are also covered.

Rescue Techniques: Instruction includes basic lifesaving methods of "reach, throw, row and go," including equipment designed for reaching and throwing from a patrol boat. The session also covers dangers from wind and propellers.

The instructor describes hazards of the "go" option, as well as the officer's swimming ability and amount of lifesaving experience and training. This session also covers other subjects, such as disrobing, water entries, floating/swimming devices, lines, rear approaches, wrist grabs, hair and collar grabs, talk and lead techniques, and the positive and negative consequences and defenses for each. Underwater removal of unconscious victims and dangers of spinal injuries are also covered.

Students learn the "instinctive drowning response" via a videotape by Doctor Pia.

The purposes of this stage are to prevent "double drownings," by allowing officers to be able to rescue victims, within their skill level. This minimizes the danger to themselves. Also, self-rescue is vital for a watercraft officer.

Stage 2: In-Water Safety Instruction (three hours)

Figure 7. Hands-on exercises greatly improve a student's learning. This class is preparing to undergo the water rescue portion of the course.

This is a series of practical exercises in a swimming pool or controlled water environment. A certified lifeguard should be present during this phase of the course, which begins with a brief five-minute stretching (warmup) exercise session. All students go through the exercises fully clothed (old pants, shirt, and shoes. Instructors should admonish them to wear a swimming suit underneath!). Students conduct each exercise after an instructor demonstration of the proper techniques.

Exercise one: Each student practices disrobing drills.

Figure 8. Each officer falls into the pool wearing an old uniform and a weight belt to simulate the gun belt. A certified lifeguard must be present in case anyone panics. Experiencing this problem in a controlled environment may save a life in a real situation.

Exercise two: Each student is equipped with a 20-pound weight belt. Kneeling next to the deep end, parallel to the side of the pool, the student falls into the water. He must surface and then release the weight belt. After dropping the weight belt, the student swims to the other side of the pool and exits. A minimum of two safety people must be in the water so as to keep the student under constant observation in case of panic.

Exercise three: In deep water, each student individually disrobes and exits the water.

Exercise four: In deep water, each practices treading water, long distance survival stroke, and surface dives.

Exercise five: Students practice water entries (slip, low and high jumps).

Figure 9. Falling overboard with clothes and weights, performing exercises in deep water, and donning various PFDs in deep water all simulate real-life conditions. A student enters the water while a lifeguard and the author oversee his safety.

Exercise six: Students practice reach and throw techniques of water rescue. Victim students in water wear PFDs, while other students "reach" with a boat hook, and "throw" with a ring buoy and line, and with a throw bag.

Figure 10. Students practice the "reach" technique of water rescue on each other.

Figure 11. Each student officer practices tossing a throw bag to a simulated victim.

Exercise seven: Students execute a surface dive and retrieve a 50-pound weight from the bottom of the pool.

Figure 12. Water safety instructors discuss the fine points of PFD placement with student officers.

Exercise eight: In deep water, students don Type I, II, and III PFDs and float in them. Students also don Type IV float coats, or survival suits, and go into water wearing them. If the float coat has a groin protector, the student must install that while in the water, as well as deploying the hood.

Figure 13. Students must learn to put on different types of PFDs while in deep water.

Exercise nine: Students practice removing an injured victim from the water.

Exercise ten: In shallow water, student teams place a victim on a back board, immobilize spine, and remove victim from water.

Safety Considerations:

This course must be taught in a pool or other clear, calm water. If a student panics, murky water deeper than ten or fifteen feet will hinder rescue. Before starting, instructors should ask students how well they swim, or if they can swim at all. This point is crucial, as some candidates cannot swim! No one should participate in the in-water exercises if he feels uncomfortable. Instructors must be proficient swimmers. This course must have a certified lifeguard or water safety instructor to oversee the pool exercises.

Figure 14. A swimming pool provides a clear, controlled training environment. Murky and uncontrolled water makes a rescue effort very difficult, if not impossible. Student officers are watching an instructor demonstrate a technique of inflating clothing with air in order to provide flotation.

Special Logistics:

Twenty-pound weight belts, 50-pound weight, various types and numbers of PFDs, "reach" and "throw" devices, videotape, handouts, a pool, and certified lifeguards and handouts are all needed for this course. This course is designed for several exercises to be conducted at the same time. There must be enough instructors (four plus lifeguard) to accommodate this. Completing this course within the time limit requires concurrent multiple exercises.

DAY FIVE

Title: WATERCRAFT OPERATION
Length: 10 Hours
Objectives:

To be able to trailer watercraft and back boat successfully for launch. To be able to rig watercraft for patrol work and operate watercraft under various adverse conditions. To be able to perform boarding maneuvers.

Description:

This is a complete hands-on course covering all aspects of watercraft operation from trailering to preparing a patrol boat for duty. Trailering and operational exercises give the student practical skills and help improve performance. The following material is from the Arizona Game and Fish Department, Lesson Plan, "Watercraft Operation," by Don Turner, November, 1988.

Stage 1: Rigging Patrol Watercraft (one hour)

This stage takes place at a trailered patrol watercraft as a lecture/demonstration, discussing the indicated item and the proper way to rig and stow each. Items to cover include: bow safety chain, spare tire lock, bow winch and line, transom tie-downs, transom saver, radio and PA system, signaling devices, first-aid kits, back board, boarding lights, enforcement marking styles, kill switch, bilge pump, sea anchor, anchor and rode, bow line, dock lines, fenders, external battery connection, battery selector switch, strobe light and cover, bilge plug, stowage of lines, PFDs, riot gun, and other enforcement equipment. Instructor shall demonstrate checking the prop for lines and stringers.

Stage 2: Trailering (three hours)

All trailering exercises (except number one) have the back window of the vehicle blacked out. Four of the exercises, two through five, run concurrently. Each exercise has its own instructor who assists the students and prepares an exercise evaluation, for a minimum of four instructors.

Exercise one: Instructors discuss the following points: hitching and safety chains and light connections; manual and surge brakes, and safety connections; trail over; backing techniques including the use of mirrors, placement of hands on the steering wheel, limited visibility, safety of the public. A demonstration will be held with the vehicle, trailer and boat parked on an inclined ramp. The instructor will explain and demonstrate how to use the engine and emergency brake for a smooth pullout.

Figure 15. This sheriff's vehicle is being used by a student to learn the proper techniques for hitching onto a trailer.

Exercise two: Student backs towing vehicle up to parked trailer, sets hitch on ball, and hooks up safety equipment. He then disconnects and pulls vehicle forward for next student.

Figure 16. Students must drive a vehicle and trailer through an obstacle course. This teaches them the very important principle of "trail over" on objects (pylons), which is much cheaper than denting a citizen's BMW!

Exercise three: Student drives vehicle, trailer, and boat through pylons (10) set in straight line, turns around and comes through to starting point. Turns around and sets up vehicle for next student.

Figure 17. Under the watchful eyes of an instructor, students must maneuver a boat and vehicle through a backing course. The instructor provides helpful tips, criticisms, and evaluations of the student's performance.

Figure 18. This student is backing his patrol boat into the right arm of the backing "cross." Not only must students handle a trailer well in reverse, but this exercise cannot be successfully completed until the student learns how to "set up" his rig for the next maneuver.

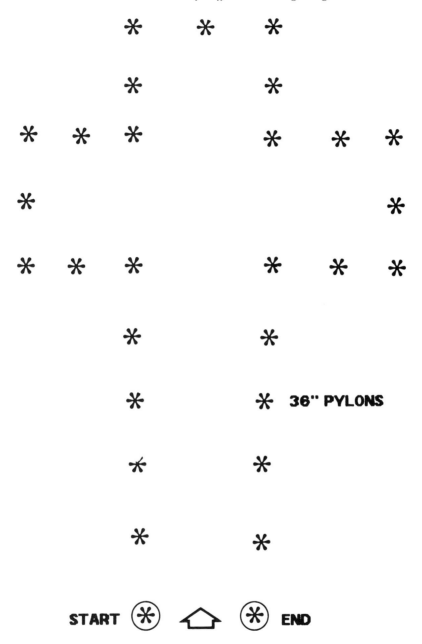

Figure 19. Boat and Trailer Backing Course.

Exercise four: This course is designed for a vehicle towing a 20′ patrol boat and uses 36″ pylons for maximum visibility. Pylons are arranged in a large open cross formation with the long end (40 yards) opened to the vehicle. Spacing is five yards at the beginning, and the pylons gradually open to eight yards at the crossbar. The crossbar begins 40 yards from the starting point and consists of two rows of pylons eight yards apart, extending 15 yards to each side. Starting point is between two pylons at the narrow (5-yard) end. Overall length of the long arm of the course is 53 yards.

Student pulls vehicle and boat forward into backing course to end of pylons. Student then backs boat and trailer to the end of the left arm of the cross. He pulls boat forward into end of cross, then backs into right arm. Boat is pulled again into the end of the cross and finally backed out the length of the cross.

Exercise five: On steep ramp, student backs boat between four pylons to edge of water. Student will stop and turn off vehicle, get out of truck, walk to rear of boat, return to truck, start vehicle and smoothly pull vehicle up incline to start.

Figure 20. With the rear window blacked out, this student is completing his launch ramp exercise. Launching a boat safely from a crowded public ramp is a necessary skill for a watercraft officer.

Figure 21. An instructor explains watercraft docking techniques to two student officers. All officers wear PFDs during water exercises.

Stage 3. Operation (four hours).

This stage requires one instructor per two students. Instructors will teach students the various handling techniques through description, demonstration and hands-on assistance, and evaluate each student's performance. Boarding maneuvers will be performed on buoys preset for this exercise. Each boat will have its own buoy.

Exercise one: Pre-launch preparation. Bow-to-stern check: disconnect trailer lights, unhook bow safety chain, remove trailering cover, power up boat, transom saver and tie-downs, bilge plug, fuel lines, equipment check, safety items check.

Figure 22. A small fleet of patrol boats, instructors and students prepares for the day's exercises. Logistical support for this course is complex, because it requires one instructor for every two students, and support equipment.

Exercise two: Launch boat; one-officer and two-officer launchings. Cold start with choke, and proper way to remove from trailer.

Exercise three: Students learn controls, gauges, and equipment. Topics to cover while on the water: Relationship of engine to pivot of boat, planing speed, use of trim, optimum cruising speed and trim, crossing wakes and waves, turns, overtaking, head-on encounters and danger zone. At idle speed, instructors will cover: beaching techniques, normal turning radius, turning in confined areas, use of reverse for stopping, maneuvering and turning skills. When operating in current, instructors will cover: beaching techniques, effects of current on maneuvering, drifting dangers, water depth reading.

Figure 23. This student is practicing approach and boarding techniques on a buoy provided for this purpose. Mistakes are easily forgiven when practicing with inexpensive objects. After their confidence and ability has improved, students will stop and board boats with simulated violations.

Exercise four: Student will handle the boat and successfully complete the following exercises: bow-on boardings, port boardings, starboard boardings. Instructors will alternate all three movements until student demonstrates proficiency. On all successful boarding maneuvers, student will approach buoy, touch it gently with boat and then hold boat in position. Student will then depart without striking buoy.

Figure 24. Students must repeat the boarding exercises until they show skill in three basic maneuvers.

Exercise five: After demonstrating proficiency with buoy, student will perform dockside maneuvers. Instructor will cover approach, departure, control of wake, approach under rough conditions.

Exercise six: Student will perform low- and medium-speed figure eights, and high-speed runs. Student will demonstrate proper trim and cruising techniques.

Exercise seven: Student will trailer boat and prepare boat for transport. Student will trailer and launch boat until he demonstrates proficiency. One-officer and two-officer trailering techniques will be covered.

Special Considerations:

Lunch will be in the field. Make arrangements for delivery of sack lunches and appropriate beverages to the training site. Instructors will prepare evaluations for each student's performance on each exercise. Students will be coached during these events.

Safety Considerations:

Students and instructors will wear PFDs for all on-water exercises. To ensure public safety, both trailering and operation exercises should take place in secure areas without public access.

Special Logistics:

This course requires a heavy commitment of equipment and instructors. The instructor-student ratio is 1:2, and each instructor must have a patrol boat and vehicle. Evaluation sheets, clipboards, pens, pylons, dock, boarding practice buoys, PFDs, sunscreen, eye protection, drinking water, and sack lunches are all required for the course.

DAY SIX

Title: WATERCRAFT TACTICAL TECHNIQUES
Length: 10 hours
Objectives:

Upon completion of this section, the watercraft officer will be able to board watercraft safely for inspections and make arrests using both the one-officer and two-officer technique. Execute stops at planing speeds. Properly seize, inventory, tow and impound watercraft. Execute high-risk water contacts using proper risk-reduction techniques for one-and two-officer patrols. Execute physical arrests on cooperative and uncooperative subjects with proper techniques for prisoner transport and security.

Description:

This course concerns itself with tactical and officer survival tips, and practical exercises. This material is taken from Arizona Game and Fish Department, Lesson Plan, "Watercraft Tactical Techniques," by Don Turner, October 1988.

Stage 1: Watercraft Officer Survival (four hours)

Through team teaching and multi-media techniques, students absorb a tactical discussion centering around watercraft officer survival and personal survival gear (See Part II, Watercraft Officer Survival as reference). Besides providing survival tips, instructors must help the students develop a survival attitude.

Officer survival training is personal. It directly relates to an officer's ability to take care of himself. The main point for officer survival is not what the student has learned but how much has he taken to heart.

Successful survival training must bridge the gap between physical skills and knowledge. Officer survival is a sixth sense, an awareness of potential threats, and situations that "feel" wrong. Often, the officer's attitude about his surrounding environment, and felt dangers, will make the difference in his ability to master the situation.

TACTICAL WORKSHEET
Apply tactics from the list in the left column and
overcome tactical degrading factors from the list at the right. Select
tactics as they are appropriate to your assigned scenario.

Tactics	Situations/scenarios: Who-when-where-how-what-why?	Degrading Factors
MISSION		
		Carelessness
INFORMATION		
		Failure to communicate
TERRAIN		
Cover		Failure to control
Concealment		subject/scene
High ground		
Distance		Failure to plan ahead
Weather		
Lighting conditions		Disregard for personal safety: (Tombstone Courage)
Noise		
LOGISTICS		
Equipment		
Vehicles		
Communication		
Firearms		
Weapons	Plan:	
PERSONNEL		
Command responsibility		
Planning		
Defense		
Offense		
Mental preparation		
Physical preparation		

Placing officers in situations that replicate deadly situations, without actually endangering them, is the basis of many officer survival exercises. Without a correct mental attitude, however, exercises will not turn knowledge into skill.

In order to emphasize the mental side of officer survival, I designed a survival exercise which taxes mental attitudes. In a group discussion, students learn that tactics are resources that an officer uses to gain the advantage and to dominate a situation from a position of strength and safety.

Students discuss various positive resources they can use to assist them. These resources come from the environment and from their equipment, training, and mental attitude. They also discuss officer errors, which can degrade chances for survival. These involve the five deadly sins of officer survival.

After this discussion, the instructor distributes a tactical training matrix, called the "Tactical Worksheet," to each student. In the left column are listed "positive factors" (tactics) which may be available to the officer for his survival. On the right column are listed "degrading factors," which work against survival.

The instructor presents a scenario, and students must prepare officer survival tactics based on their positive and negative factors. Students work best in small groups, and each group should have a different situation. When finished, each group explains to the class how they used their positive resources to work the scenario and how they overcame the degrading factors.

This exercise always generates lively discussions. Its purpose is to make the students think about what they can use to survive, with the hope that they will develop more tactical awareness of their patrol area and personal resources.

Figure 25. For the tactical course, students are paired with an instructor. Students in this group discuss various exercises they will complete, while an instructor explains felony stop procedures to his two students. In order to add realism, students wear their uniforms and are issued "dummy" guns.

Stage 2: Day Tactics (four hours)

Two students are paired with each instructor and a patrol boat. Based on team working requirements, a work team with its own boat is the best arrangement. Students will be in work uniform and instructors will issue dummy guns.

Exercise one: In a central area, instructors demonstrate the proper way to perform a high-speed felony stop, felony boarding, felony arrest tactics, and seizure and towing techniques. Instructors also demonstrate the proper techniques for slow-speed misdemeanor citations and a dockside boating safety inspection.

Hands-on demonstrations should allow the students a theater view of the enactment. An experienced instructor should describe the events as they unfold, enumerating the various steps the players take to protect themselves from the "suspects." The demonstration provides students with an overview, giving them an understanding of the overall tactical situation. This lays the groundwork for students to run through their own scenarios correctly.

Figure 26. Two instructor officers demonstrate proper felony boarding techniques on two instructor suspects.

Exercise two: Working as a two-officer patrol unit, students perform a high-speed felony stop, using proper techniques from suspect recognition to seizure and towing of suspect vessel.

Exercise three: Working as a one-officer unit, each student performs a slow-speed misdemeanor stop ending in citation for an unannounced violation on subject's boat. Instructor/subjects will create a violation and the student must discover it and take appropriate enforcement action.

Exercise four: Working alone, each student performs a complete dockside boating safety inspection.

Figure 27. This officer performs a complete dockside boating safety inspection while others observe.

Figure 28. Practical exercises include night operations.

Stage 3: Night Tactics (2 hours)

For this stage, students are again paired with an instructor and patrol boat but not the same instructor as during the day exercises.

Exercise one: Student operates patrol boat at slow speed and high speed at night.

Figure 29. A suspect's point of view of a student and his instructor conducting a night-boarding drill.

Exercise two: Operating as a two-officer patrol, each team performs a night approach to an anchored subject watercraft. Instructor/subjects are to be verbally abusive and are to be in violation. Students will have to determine the violation and issue citation(s) while keeping control of the scene. The evaluating instructor must watch carefully, because the emotional pitch of the exercise can be quite high. He will terminate the exercise if it progresses beyond verbal abuse or if students escalate the contact.

Figure 30. Good role playing on the part of the instructor/suspects greatly enhances the realism of the exercise to the student.

Figure 31. Weapons control is extremely important. A student checks in his revolver. A safety instructor receives the guns and locks the unloaded firearms in a safe locker and then issues each student a dummy gun. Instructors on each boat inspect pockets and loaders for ammunition. The pile of guns in front of the student are dummy ones waiting to be issued. Their color is international orange to provide immediate safety recognition.

Safety Considerations:

Students and instructors will have only dummy "red-handled" firearms, including a long gun available as well as sidearms. Instructor/subjects should have a variety of firearms.

Before boarding for the exercises, a safety instructor should personally inspect every student and instructor for firearms and ammunition. NO BACKUP OR HIDE–OUT GUNS ARE ALLOWED. Watercraft shall be inspected and all weapons removed. Officers are not to wear batons, nor carry chemical weapons, except for dummy or inoperative devices. Every instructor shall inspect his boat before allowing students to board, and inspect the students as they board the boats. All instructors are responsible for safety and will expel any student who fails to comply with safety regulations. This should be made quite clear to them during both the orientation and tactics lectures.

Safety issues also cover the operation of the boats. All participants will wear PFDs when on the water. During night exercises, all will wear eye protection.

Other Considerations:

There will be two types of instructors needed for this exercise: evaluating instructors and instructor/subjects. Every two students will have an evaluating instructor who will complete a student evaluation form for each hands-on exercise. These evaluations will serve to fulfill the "test" portion of each course and will cover knowledge of the watercraft laws, agency procedures, watercraft operation and officer survival skills. Evaluating instructors are not part of the actual exercise, as their role is to evaluate student skills and to critique each student after each exercise.

The evaluating instructor is in charge of the students and exercise. One of his duties is to ensure officer and instructor safety, with the authority to curtail an exercise if it appears to be unsafe or is getting out of control.

As part of the instructor's evaluation, he will also recommend a "pass/fail" score for the student. Students who fail may have an opportunity to repeat the exercise if the instructor feels the student's performance can improve. If the instructor feels that the student will not benefit from a repeat of the exercise, he informs the chief instructor, who is responsible for the final determination. If a student fails an exercise twice, the instructor will note that the student failed that part of the course, and the chief instructor will decide any follow-up action.

Figure 32. Instructors provide each student with constructive suggestions. This evaluation is a critical part of the training program, because without good feedback, students cannot improve their performance. A good instructor should be both a coach and an evaluator.

The student, however, shall not graduate from the watercraft school until performance is up to standard. As stated above, safety violations require automatic expulsion.

The chief instructor will conduct an instructor training course before these exercises, to brief the instructors on their duties and on the objectives of each exercise.

Instructor/subjects shall play the role of subjects and suspects. Each violator boat will have at least two instructor/subjects aboard. For two of the exercises, the instructor/subjects will set up a misdemeanor violation, changing the violation for each student. Only in certain exercises will the instructor/subjects be verbally abusive. During the felony boarding exercise, instructor/subjects will take no physical action against the students, unless the student(s) commits one of the "five deadly sins" of officer survival or uses poor tactics. Then the instructors/suspects may take any safe act against the offending student, including simulating deadly force with dummy guns or rubber knives.

Videotaping various exercises provides the student with immediate feedback on his performance. It allows the instructor to explain mistakes and fortify good tactics.

In Stage 2, Exercises two, three and four should run concurrently to save time. Likewise in Stage 3, there should be several concurrent situations for Exercise two.

Special Logistics:

This course is logistically difficult. Without enough instructors and watercraft for a two-students, one-boat, and one-instructor ratio, a staging area may be necessary for students to wait for an available boat. Arizona uses a houseboat as a student resting site. All students and instructors must have PFDs and wear them.

Instructor/subjects must have fake ID, boat registrations, fishing licenses, HINs, and WC numbers. They also need enough props to make their roles realistic. Evaluating instructors must have enough evaluation forms, pens, and fake citation books.

If you are near a base station, arrange for mock radio traffic concerning the instructor/subjects. Without this, simulation is still possible, using the boat radios and an instructor as the "dispatcher."

For coordination, there should be a chief instructor who is not part of the exercises and is thereby free to move around, oversee, and deal with problems as they arise. He should have his own boat for transportation.

All radios should be working and all boats should be able to communicate with each other. There must be marked patrol watercraft for student use and unmarked watercraft for instructor/subject use. Each student should have a dummy sidearm and each patrol boat a dummy long gun.

Arrangements for meals, drinks and restroom facilities must be prepared in advance. A logistical worksheet, with both personnel and material requirements, is mandatory.

DAY SEVEN

Title: WATERCRAFT FIREARMS
Length: Four hours
Objectives:

To properly operate a watercraft through a series of maneuvers and at high speeds while engaging hostile targets using police firearms in a tactically correct way.

Figure 33. The watercraft firearms part of this course occurs on the final day. Shooting at moving targets from an unstable platform, while practicing good officer survival techniques, is an exercise offered in only a few states.

Description:

This practical firearms course combines operational and tactical skills learned in the previous six days with shooting skills.

Stage 1: Instructor Workshop

Because of the nature of this course, prior instructor training is essential but not as part of this course. Instructor training should take a workshop format, which consists of an explanation of the course objectives, safety considerations, teaching/coaching techniques, firearms course layouts, logistics and other considerations. It should culminate with instructors completing the firing stages.

Figure 34. Author Don Turner briefs instructors on the safety procedures that are part of the watercraft firearms course.

Stage 2: Briefing (¹/₂ hour)

Students and instructors are briefed on layout of shooting course, safety considerations, safety areas, loading and unloading procedures, ammo issue procedures, the use of cover and concealment, and shooting-from-a-boat skills. This is the appropriate point to assign the boat and personnel who will paste and score targets.

Stage 3: Watercraft Tactical Firearms Course (3¹/₂ hours)

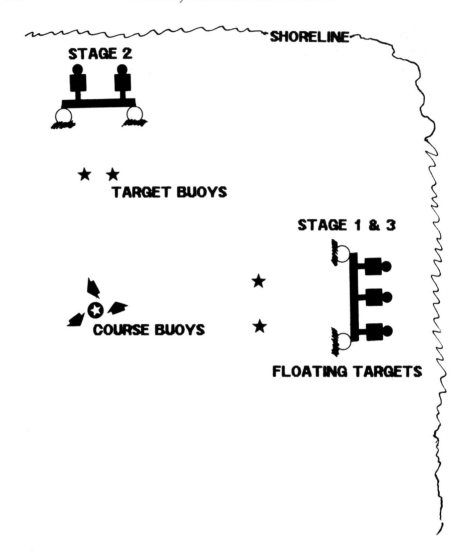

STAGE 2

★ ★
TARGET BUOYS

STAGE 1 & 3

★

★
COURSE BUOYS

FLOATING TARGETS

SHORELINE

START ✪ ⌂ ✪ END

Figure 35. Arizona Game & Fish Department Watercraft Firearms Course.

Following are three different courses and their explanations:
Course A: Arizona Game and Fish Watercraft Department Firearms
Course (adapted from Florida Marine Patrol, Tucker & Willoughby).

Dimensions may vary to suit local conditions. The distance between
the course buoy and the target buoys should be between 25 and 75
yards. Target buoys should be between 10 and 20 yards from the
targets. Targets may be floating near shore or on shore, but, either
way, a safe backstop is essential. The starting gate is between two
course buoys.

The course requires a patrol boat with an instructor and two students.
One student shoots the course at a time. Ammo issue is 18 rounds
sidearm, 4 rounds shotgun. The course has three stages. Beginning at
the starting gate, the student drives the boat, with lights and sirens,
around the center buoy. All turns around this buoy are counterclockwise.
Once around the center buoy, he goes to Stage 1, which consists of
three targets. He stops at the marker buoys and fires two shots per
target, reloads, and fires another two per target, using the gunnel as
cover for both firing and reloading. The student starts up, goes around
the center buoy again, and proceeds to Stage 2, requiring two shotgun
rounds per target. Making another turn around the center buoy, the
student approaches the three targets for Stage 3, requiring backing the
boat up to the marker buoys. After firing two shots at each target,
using the engine and transom for cover, he resumes and makes a turn
around the central buoy and finishes at the starting gate. Score is total
hits over time.

Figure 36. A student maneuvers his watercraft through the tactical firearms course while his partner hangs on. Each boat has two students and a safety officer/instructor. Students load their guns in a safe area and firearms remain "hot" throughout the course.

Figure 37. The first stage has the student firing two shots at the highest threat level target first. He then fires two rounds at each of the other two targets, reloads, and repeats the drill for a total of 12 shots.

Figure 38. After shooting, he steers the boat around a course buoy to Stage 2. As the course is scored by time and hits, speed is important here.

Figure 39. A student fires two #00 buckshot loads at each of two targets, taking out the highest threat level first. Many find that shouldering a long gun while wearing a PFD is a difficult feat.

Figure 40. A high-speed turn around a course buoy, after firing the shotgun stage, sets the student up for Stage 3.

Figure 41. The last stage consists of "double-tapping" three targets utilizing the stern and engine as cover. Watercraft handling techniques are as important as shooting skills. Failing to halt the forward progress of the boat can lead to some interesting situations.

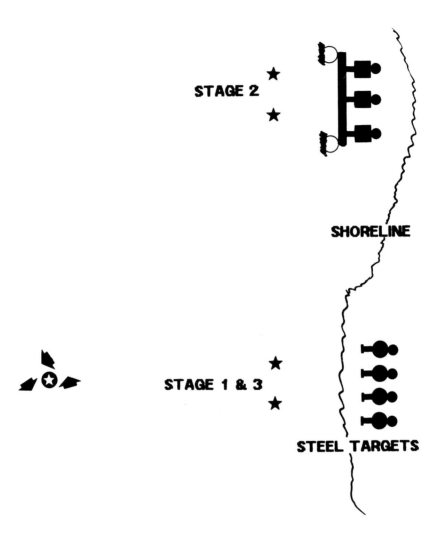

STAGE 2

SHORELINE

STAGE 1 & 3

STEEL TARGETS

Figure 42. Watercraft Tactical Firearms Course #1.

Course B: Watercraft Tactical Firearms Course #1

Dimensions of this course may vary to suit local conditions. We suggest 50 yards between the starting gate buoys and the center buoy and similar spacing between the course and target buoys. For Stages 1 and 3, target buoys should be about seven yards from the floating paper targets. Stage 2 consists of four steel "pepper poppers," on the shore, with target buoys about 20 yards from them. Safe backstops are essential. Although #00 Buck is one choice, #4 birdshot helps reduce ricochets.

Course requires a patrol boat with an instructor and two students. One student shoots the course at a time. Ammo issue is 18 rounds sidearm and four rounds shotgun. The student comes through the starting gate, goes counterclockwise around the center buoy to Stage 1, to engage three separate targets three times each (two in the chest, one in the head) from the gunnel. The student then goes clockwise around the center buoy, to Stage 2, the four "pepper poppers," to engage them with the shotgun (one shot per target) from the gunnel. He then goes around the center buoy counterclockwise and returns to the first three targets for Stage 3. This requires two shots in the chest and one shot in the head on each target, which is performed from cover behind the gunnel. Student leaves the course straight out. Score is total hits divided by time.

Figure 43. Students fire the "armored opponent" drill at Stages 1 and 3.

Course C: Watercraft Tactical Firearms Course #2

Dimensions depend on local conditions. There are four pairs of targets, anchored just off the shoreline, with a buoy 25 to 50 yards in front of and between each pair. We suggest 25 yards between the starting gate buoys and the four center course buoys, but spacing will vary between the course and target buoys. Stage 1 should have the target buoy about seven yards from the targets, and subsequent stages should require increasing ranges, up to about 25 yards. All four sets of two targets can be floating paper targets. Safe backstops are essential.

Course requires a patrol boat with an instructor and two students. One student shoots the course at a time. Ammo issue is equivalent to duty issue, but the course requires 18 rounds for the sidearm and four slug rounds for the shotgun to complete the course with no misses. Student begins by passing between two buoys as a starting gate, goes clockwise around the first buoy, and runs in to stop seven yards from and parallel to the first target pair. The student executes an "armored

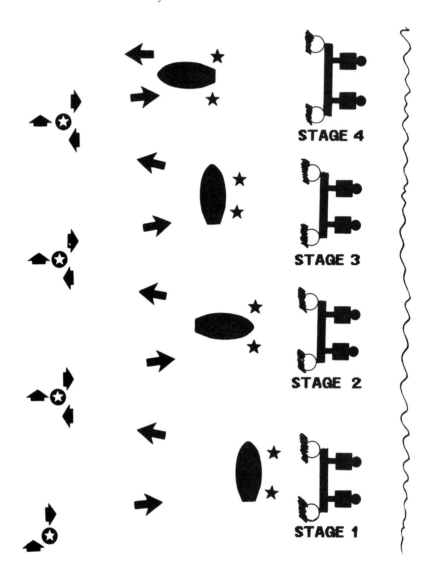

Figure 44. Watercraft Tactical Firearms Course #2.

opponent drill" against each target with his handgun, as his other hand maintains control of the helm. He starts his boat again, passes around the next buoy, and stops 15 yards from and bow in to the next target pair, where he again goes through the armored opponent drill using the bow as cover. He starts up again, goes around the next buoy, and turns parallel to the next set of targets. Using the gunnel for cover, he repeats the drill but at 20 yards distance. Upon starting up again, he goes around the last buoy and parks stern-on to the last pair, firing two shotgun slugs at each over the transom. Starting up again, he slaloms his boat through the line of buoys and goes back through the gate. The score is mandatory hits, no bullet limitation, just total time. Tactical reloads are mandatory.

Figure 45. With the engine as cover, a "double tap" with shotgun slugs completes Watercraft Tactical Firearms Course #2.

Safety Considerations:

Instructors must be firearms instructors and identified with visible ID. We use bright orange baseball caps.

Students receive ammo only when ready to shoot. There must be an ammo safety officer and a safe area to load and unload the firearms. Students may handle firearms only when loading, unloading, or shooting.

Figure 46. There is no substitute for safety. A safe backstop is essential for conducting this course. Other safety factors include alert safety officers, strict ammo control, and a safe loading and unloading area.

All targets must have safe backstops. Keeping students in a staging area without ammunition, while waiting their turn to shoot, promotes safety. The staging area must be far enough away to be safe from ricochets.

There shall be a minimum of one safety boat per course to keep the public away. The chief instructor shall have his own boat and be primarily concerned with safety and keeping the courses running smoothly.

Figure 47. The chief instructor must have his own boat to monitor the students' and instructors' performances, as well as safety procedures.

If you have the manpower and safe areas, it may be possible to run two courses at the same time. Each course should have a scoring boat, or the boat that just completed the run should return to score. All personnel will have ear and eye protection and all officers will wear PFDs. All watercraft will have radios.

Instructors will closely supervise the shooter and any passengers on the boat. Students should load only upon command and be proficient in decocking and unloading their firearms. Instructors will watch the muzzle of the firearm and be prepared to take immediate action to prevent an accident. Other points to watch are loading and unloading firearms, holstering, the boat's drift, and anything else affecting safety. The instructor shall order a cease-fire if unsafe conditions develop. Steel targets are unsafe because the drift of the boat prevents stabilization of the ricochet angle, but using frangible bullets and birdshot reduces this risk.

Figure 48. Targets which appear realistic greatly improve the course. These Speedwell targets are life-size pictures of suspects and depict different threat levels. This complicates the student's decision making, as he must choose which threat level takes priority.

Ideally, paper targets showing different threat levels are worth using, because they don't produce ricochets. These are ideal if placed on floats with a good bank backstop. In use, students fire on the highest threat level first.

Other Considerations:

Firing from an unstable platform at a bobbing target is very different from firing on dry land. Our experience has shown that some officers who score very well in dry-land qualification courses may do poorly when required to fire under unstable water conditions.

One popular land training drill has the shooter drawing and firing two rounds each into three silhouettes, reloading and firing two shots into each of the same targets again, in reverse order, from the standing position. This drill is worse than useless for waterborne officers, because it's hopelessly optimistic to expect suspects to stand up in their boats while bullets are flying. It's also poor tactics for the officer to remain standing while shooting it out with multiple aggressors.

When designing a watercraft live fire course, it's important to remember that the instructor is dealing with experienced officers and that oversimplifying the course will detract from real-life encounters. Firearms courses should be designed for the area in which the students work and how they work. For instance, if they work one-officer patrols, their course should not emphasize two-officer tactics.

Figure 49. Instructors must maintain a constant alert for safety problems. A close eye on muzzle control will eliminate many potential dangers.

Safety is a vital concern for several reasons. One is that it's still necessary to enforce routine safety practices, such as wearing ear and eye protection. Advanced students can suffer from ear and eye injuries as well as novices. Another is that advanced firearms training is more dynamic than basic academy training or routine qualifications. Operating a patrol watercraft and firing at bobbing targets increases the chances of an accident, especially if there's more than one student aboard.

Figure 50. Police academies do not provide officers with the training necessary to successfully engage adversaries on the water. Watercraft firearms training will cause a basic academy firearms instructor to have severe heart palpations.

This can be a critical point, because our experience has been that basic academies provide only the rudiments of firearms handling. There are graduates whose only knowledge of firearms is what they learned at the academy. They can load, unload, hit stationary targets at up to 25 yards, and clean their sidearms. Basic academy training may not encompass the tactical reload, clearing jams, use of cover, and other aspects that we consider essential before an officer is ready to face the real world. This suggests that intermediate training and experience will be necessary before the student is ready for water-borne firearms training.

Figure 51. A good transition technique, from land to water, is to have students shoot while standing on an unstable platform.

One way to help students progress from dry land shooting to water is to have them shoot standing on a flat board on top of an inflated inner tube. While standing on this device, they should be shooting at a bobbing or moving target. Their session on the tube should also include reloading drills.

Students will often find that hitting a moving target from an unstable gun platform is totally different from conventional dry-land firing, and it's normal for scores to drop drastically.

Conventional firearms training has students using any available cover or concealment, both to protect themselves from suspects' fire and to stabilize their firearms. On a boat, the rules change, and trying to use the unstable boat as a gun platform is counterproductive. This is why students should not rest their hands or forearms on the gunnels.

Figure 52. A Port-A–Target bobbing target helps provide land-based training with both an unstable gun platform and a moving target.

Live-fire courses should include all the guns the officers are allowed to carry. The live-fire course must be a tactical course, not just another exercise. What makes a course "tactical?" It must cover the following points:

1. It's tactically sound. Participants are required to follow good tactics, such as using cover and cross-fire. They are also not to do anything that would be bad tactics in the real world.

2. The course is not standardized or stereotyped. There should always be some surprise, instead of a routine set of shooting exercises that officers soon learn by rote. The course should be different every time, and students learn only the rough outline in the briefing. This is important as Burg points out, because in real life officers don't follow scripted challenges.[1]

3. Students face problems, not just targets. A row of silhouettes is not much of a challenge and requires no problem-solving ability. Real-life suspects won't be standing in a neat row for the officer's convenience. Using several photographic targets, representing various threat levels, requires the officer to assign priority, not simply shoot in a pattern. Having one or more targets partially obstructed is another challenge, and the officer must decide to shoot first and then seek cover, or vice versa.

Another aspect is integrating problems with the firing course. An instructor can cause the student problems that are similar to those he might face on duty and which he must overcome. Instructors Tucker and Willoughby, of the Florida Marine Patrol, fire a blank gun over the head of their students if they don't take proper cover, for instance. Instructors can issue non-functional rounds mixed with live rounds, giving students a malfunction while trying to finish a course.

Students should also have to learn to fire handguns with one hand, instead of always relying on the two-handed grip currently stressed in police training. The reason is that the officer may have to use one hand to control the helm or to hang on to the boat in rough water. An officer without one-hand firing experience may be unable to hit an adversary if required to do so in a real-life problem.

Students who wear eyeglasses need to know how they perform without them. The instructor may require the student to replace them with uncorrected safety glasses. Burg points out that an officer may be involved in a fight before having to draw his sidearm, and that knowing how he'll perform without them has practical value, as well as providing points for legal defense if a shooting incident goes to court.[2]

4. Scoring is also based on the use of tactics, not just raw number of hits. Students can fail if they do anything so tactically unsound that it would have put them in serious danger of being killed or injured, such as reloading without using cover. Safety violations are a sure ticket for being dismissed from the course. Students should use whatever cover or concealment is available on the patrol boat. Even with a low gunnel, students should try to make small targets of themselves and should pay special attention to reducing their profiles while reloading. Instructors should note if the student maintains eye contact with the target while reloading and makes best use of available cover and concealment.

A set of targets requiring use of the long gun should also be part of the course. If the firearm is a shotgun, the range should be longer than

Figure 53. Watercraft training is dynamic instruction and requires extensive logistical planning. For instance, navigational aids personnel set the buoys used in the watercraft operations and firearms courses. Without good logistical planning, the best course will be a dud.

that for the handgun. If the agency authorizes rifles, ranges can be much greater.

Ammunition issue for each course depends upon course tactics. The conventional way is to issue a specified number of rounds and count their hits. The second way is to allow officers to carry their normal duty complement and require a specific number of successful hits on each target. This forces the student to concentrate upon accomplishing his task, not just making quick time and firing a limited number of rounds. It adds realism because the officer must take more care in aiming. It also places a heavier responsibility upon the instructor, who must assure that the student surrenders all surplus rounds upon finishing the stage.

Firing from watercraft can bring hazards that dry-land officers never face. Officers with auto pistols must be careful not to drop their magazine into the water during reloading. Other hazards involve poor boat operation, as in running the boat aground, fouling the prop in the buoy lines, or failing to stop the boat at a shooting station.

Figure 54. It's necessary to design and build targets. Instructors should set up the course early enough to avoid keeping students waiting. Everything must be ready when the course begins.

Figure 55. In order to save labor costs, students can perform some support activities. They can act as suspects or, as in this picture, they can help to paste and score targets.

Watercraft firing courses require intensive supervision, because the situation is dynamic. It's easier for shots to go wild, endangering others. Instructors must ensure that students keep their firearms pointed in a safe direction, by direct physical intervention if necessary.

Special Logistics:

This is another logistically complicated course. A logistical worksheet is mandatory. Instructors shall preview the area and locate safe places for the targets and boats to operate. Any local and or state-required permits must be procured well in advance of the training. Ammunition must be calculated and ordered in advance. Targets and other accessories, as well as backup eye and ear protection must not be forgotten. Items necessary for the welfare of the students, including drinks, meals and toilet facilities, and a staging area all require planning.

A realistic firing course can be great fun and a tremendous learning experience.

NOTES:

1. Burg, Sgt. Mike, *Firearms Training Courses: Make 'em Real, Law and Order,* November, 1989, pp. 93–94.
2. Ibid., pp. 93–94.

Chapter 25

ADVANCED WATERCRAFT PATROL OFFICER TRAINING

Advanced training begins where special schools end. This type of training emphasizes specific techniques too difficult to master during specialized courses. Typically, only the "advanced" student will attend these classes.

Every subject can have advanced courses. These skill improvement classes will only be limited by imagination and money. We won't even attempt to try to list all the advanced courses that are possible. We present a few advanced training course suggestions, to outline some possibilities.

Advanced firearms will concentrate on complex shooting decisions, team shooting tactics, triad shoots (pistol, rifle, shotgun), automatic weapons, role playing, and other advanced tactics.

Watercraft tactics will include ramming techniques, evasion maneuvers, high-speed stopping techniques, multiple patrol boat boarding tactics, aerial support, advanced rescue, and various other advanced skills.

Everyone can get stale. We suggest that you constantly keep yourself refreshed and current on officer survival tactics. Learn new ways of doing something better and then pass on your ideas to others. We wish you the best of luck in your work, and may you arrive at the end of your shift safely.

INDEX

A

Accident investigation, 23, 24, 93, 141, 147, 196, 212
Accident Investigation Kit, 141
Accidents, 13, 14, 15, 19, 24, 87, 92, 158, 172, 212
Aeronautical charts, 92
Aircraft, 99, 133, 178, 179
Alcohol, 14, 15, 16, 51, 53, 75, 108, 111, 112, 115, 213, 214
Alcohol consumption, 14, 15, 16, 45, 55
Alphabet recitation, 16
Altered or obliterated HINs, 22
Ambush, 120, 131, 132, 133
Ammunition, 124, 126, 133, 150, 189, 243, 258, 266, 268
Archaeological site preservation, 26
Arrests, 16, 59, 73, 83, 150, 210, 235
ASP collapsible baton, 49
Assaults, 23, 39, 119, 120, 121, 130, 196
Attacks, 119, 120, 129
Attitude, 35, 36, 43, 51, 65, 122, 129, 130, 198, 235, 237
Auto-knives, 148

B

Back-up gun, 150
Back-up officer, 58
Batons, 49, 106, 121, 145, 147, 152, 185, 196, 243
Batteries, 39, 63, 128, 140, 142, 160, 161, 176
Bilge plugs, 49, 163
Binoculars, 55, 70, 97, 98, 146, 147
Blood alcohol level, 15, 16
Boarding inspections, 40
Boarding ladders, 63, 109, 164
Boardings, 66, 99, 167, 185, 233

Boater sobriety check points, 16
Boating accidents, 31
Boating collisions, 11, 15
Boating fatalities, 13
Boating safety inspection, 23, 25, 56, 65, 67, 239
Body armor, 128, 149, 150
Booby traps, 64, 84, 105, 106
Brooks, Pierce, 36
Buckshot, 124, 127
Bullet penetration, 126, 127
Burg, Sgt. Mike, 264, 265, 269

C

Campgrounds, 23, 26, 51, 53, 88, 98, 115
Canteen, 138
CAP–STUN, 148
Carbine, 125, 151
Chemical control agents, 121, 148
Citation Book, 144
Clarke, General Bruce, 29
Complacency, 27, 163
Concealed weapons, 26
Contact officer, 41, 57, 58, 59, 60, 78, 79, 80
Contraband, 22, 68, 77, 84
Coordination tests, 15, 16
Countermeasures, 58, 121, 130, 131, 196
Cover and concealment, 125, 128, 192, 247
Cover officer, 78, 79, 80, 83, 99, 184
Cross-fire, 264
Cyalume Light Sticks, 140

D

Deadly force, 121, 130, 196, 244
Defensive Tactics, 121
Dehydration, 15, 111, 138
Disabled boats, 62

273

Dive platforms, 63
Dog leash, 143
Drowning, 31, 88, 107, 108, 218
Drug smuggling, 8, 22, 105
Drugs, 14, 16, 22, 51, 53, 75, 214

E

Edged weapons, 121
Empty-hand techniques, 121
Environmental factors, 35, 58
Evidence kit, 140
External battery terminals, 160

F

Felony boarding, 57, 61, 77, 102, 238
Felony stop, 75, 83, 102, 238, 239
Finger counting, 16
First aid, 31, 88, 90, 92, 110
First aid kit, 173, 175
First responder kit, 174
Fishermen marker buoys, 102
Flares, 91, 92, 102, 140, 177, 178, 186
Flashlight, 39, 85, 100, 106, 121, 142, 145, 146, 152, 153, 196
Float coat, 100, 108, 114, 139, 222
Florida Marine Patrol, 78

G

Game warden, 25, 105
Gun belt, 75, 83, 88, 89, 90, 108, 112, 113, 123, 140, 146, 147, 149, 152, 186

H

Hand signals, 41, 42
Handcuffing, 74, 75, 76, 78, 80, 85, 191, 196
Handcuffs, 80, 83, 142, 143, 152
Handgun, 78, 127, 131, 133, 205, 257, 265, 266
Helicopter, 87, 89, 90, 91, 140, 178, 179
HGN (Horizontal Gaze Nystagmus), 16, 28
High speed approaches, 59, 73
High speed pursuits, 61
High-risk boardings, 78, 99, 196
HIN (Hull Identification Numbers), 11, 12, 21, 22, 67, 71, 146, 212, 245
Hunters, 25, 26, 121

Hypothermia, 66, 89, 108, 109, 110, 111, 113, 139, 171, 196, 217

I

Impaired operators, 15
Impairment tests, 16
Instinctive drowning response, 107, 172, 218
Instructor cadre, 198, 199
Intoximeters, 16, 197, 214

J

Jordan, Bill, 133
Juveniles, 45, 49, 52, 196

K

Kersey, Sgt. Gerald, 16
Kill switch, 63, 75, 100, 112, 163, 170, 225
Kill zone, 131, 132
Knife, 119, 122, 130, 147, 148, 152
Kubotan, 121, 146, 147

L

Lanyard, 100, 163, 170
Liability, 67, 73, 97, 202, 203
Logistics, 29, 197, 198, 200, 201, 202, 205, 208, 212, 213, 214, 216, 217, 224, 235, 236, 245, 246, 268

M

Mini-flashlight, 76, 146, 176
Moving target, 131, 263

N

NASBLA, 196
Night operations, 95, 96, 97, 100, 109, 140, 162, 182, 186
Noise regulations, 14, 29
Nylon gear, 152

O

Officer Donald L. Holland, 41
Ohio Division of Wildlife, 42
One-man patrols, 39, 49, 57
Operating Under the Influence, 14, 16, 214

P

Patrol Evaluations, 29
Personal weapons, 119, 120, 121
PFDs, (Personal Flotation Devices) 13, 23, 40,
    65, 88, 89, 109, 116, 120, 171, 172, 215,
    217, 220, 222, 224, 225, 234, 235, 243, 245,
    259
Pia, Dr. Frank, 19, 107, 108, 109, 218
Pike poles, 88
Pistols, 26, 42, 122, 126, 133, 266, 271
Poachers, 101, 128
Positive attitude, 35
Prisoner Transport, 83
Probable cause, 22, 55
Prohibited weapons, 26
Public-address system, 56

R

Radios, 42, 50, 71, 97, 245, 259
Reckless operation, 14, 17
Recreational boating, 5, 6, 21, 22, 25, 35
Revolvers, 122, 126, 133, 206
Rifle, 1, 49, 78, 124, 125, 126, 127, 131, 133, 151,
    185, 191, 196, 197, 201, 266, 271
Ring buoys, 88, 172, 220
Riot gun, 23, 42, 49, 150, 185. Also see
    "Shotgun."
Routine patrol, 27, 28, 29

S

Safety equipment, 12, 13, 14
Safety equipment inspections, 11, 12, 13
Saturation Patrols, 28
Scabbards, 49, 125
Scott, Jerry, 35, 42, 130
Search and Rescue, 8, 31, 102, 195
Second gun, 150
Security Strap, 143
Selective Enforcement Patrols, 28, 29
Shore-line contacts, 45, 48, 49, 50
Shot bags, 57, 168
Shotgun, 26, 41, 42, 78, 123, 124, 125, 131, 150,
    151, 196, 205, 249, 254, 255, 257, 265, 271.
    Also see "Riot Gun."
Side-handle baton, 49
Signal mirror, 140, 178

Smugglers, 22, 128
Sound Meter, 19
Special patrols, 29
Speed-loaders, 152
Spotlight, 91, 97, 100, 117
Stolen boats, 21, 22, 69, 70
Strobe light, 100, 113, 140, 176, 225
Stun guns, 150
Sunblock, 138, 206, 208
Sunglasses, 97, 137
Survival attitude, 35
Survival suit, 100, 108, 110, 111, 114, 123, 139,
    222
Survival tactics, 35, 51, 74, 93, 237, 271
Survival triangle, 35

T

Tactical Worksheet, 236, 237
Theft, 21, 22, 23, 26, 70, 158, 163
Throw bag, 88, 172, 220
Towing, 12, 17, 62, 80, 84, 115, 116, 117, 155,
    156, 157, 158, 159, 187, 197, 226, 229, 238,
    239
Trailering, 158, 159, 197, 225, 231, 234
Transport belt, 83, 144
Trolling motor, 58, 160, 185
Tucker, Captain Mike, 19, 78, 249, 265
Two-man patrol, 39, 50, 57, 67

U

U.S. Coast Guard, 6, 13, 21
Use-of-force policies, 121

V

Verbal control techniques, 121

W

Willoughby, Capt. Ken, 19, 78, 249, 265